SEMINAR STUDIES IN HISTORY
General Editor: Roger Lockyer

The Age
of Discovery
1400–1550

Dan O'Sullivan

LONGMAN
London and New York

LONGMAN GROUP LIMITED
Longman House, Burnt Mill, Harlow, Essex, CM20 2JE, England
and Associated Companies throughout the World.
Published in the United States of America
by Longman Inc., New York

First published 1984
ISBN 0 582 35372 6

Set in 10/11pt. Baskerville, Linotron 202.

*Printed in Hong Kong by
Commonwealth Printing Press Ltd*

British Library Cataloguing in Publication Data

O'Sullivan, Dan
   The age of discovery 1400–1550. —
   (Seminar studies in history)
   1. Discoveries (in geography)   2. Explorers
   — History
   I. Title   II. Series
   910'.9'024   G175

   ISBN 0-582-35372-6

Library of Congress Cataloging in Publication Data

O'Sullivan, Dan.
   The Age of Discovery, 1440–1550.

   (Seminar studies in history)
   Bibliography: p.
   Includes index.
   1. America — Discovery and exploration.   2. Navigation —
Europe — History.   I. Title.   II. Series.
E101.088 1984   970.01   83-9886
ISBN 0-582-35372-6

Contents

Acknowledgements

We are grateful to the following for permission to reproduce copyright material:

Hakluyt Society, London for extracts from *The Chronicles of the Discovery and Conquest of Guinea: vol. I* by G. E. Azurara, *Europeans in West Africa: vol. I* by Joao de Barros (1942), *First Voyage of Vasco da Gama* Ed. E. G. Ravenstein (1898), *Journal of Christopher Columbus during his First Voyage* Ed. C. R. Markham (1893), *The Letters of Amerigo Vespucci* Ed. C. R. Markham (1894), *Magellan's First Voyage round the World* Trans. Lord Stanley of Alderney (1874), *Mandeville's Travels: vol. I, Reports on the Discovery of Peru* Ed. C. R. Markham (1872), *The True History of the Conquest of New Spain: vols I, II and IV* by Bernal Diaz del Castillo (1908, 1910 and 1912) and *The Voyages of Cadamosta* Ed. G. R. Crone (1937); Walker & Co. Inc., for extracts from *The European Reconnaissance* by J. H. Parry (1968)

Cover: Engraving by F. H. Bruegel of a sixteenth century Carrack leaving port. National Maritime Museum, London.

Seminar Studies in History

Founding Editor: Patrick Richardson

Introduction

The Seminar Studies series was conceived by Patrick Richardson, whose experience of teaching history persuaded him of the need for something more substantial than a textbook chapter but less formidable than the specialised full-length academic work. He was also convinced that such studies, although limited in length, should provide an up-to-date and authoritative introduction to the topic under discussion as well as a selection of relevant documents and a comprehensive bibliography.

Patrick Richardson died in 1979, but by that time the Seminar Studies series was firmly established, and it continues to fulfil the rôle he intended for it. This book, like others in the series, is therefore a living tribute to a gifted and original teacher.

Note on the System of References:
A bold number in round brackets (**5**) in the text refers the reader to the corresponding entry in the Bibliography section at the end of the book. A bold number in square brackets, preceded by 'doc' [**doc 6**] refers the reader to the corresponding items in the section of Documents, which follows the main text.

ROGER LOCKYER
General Editor

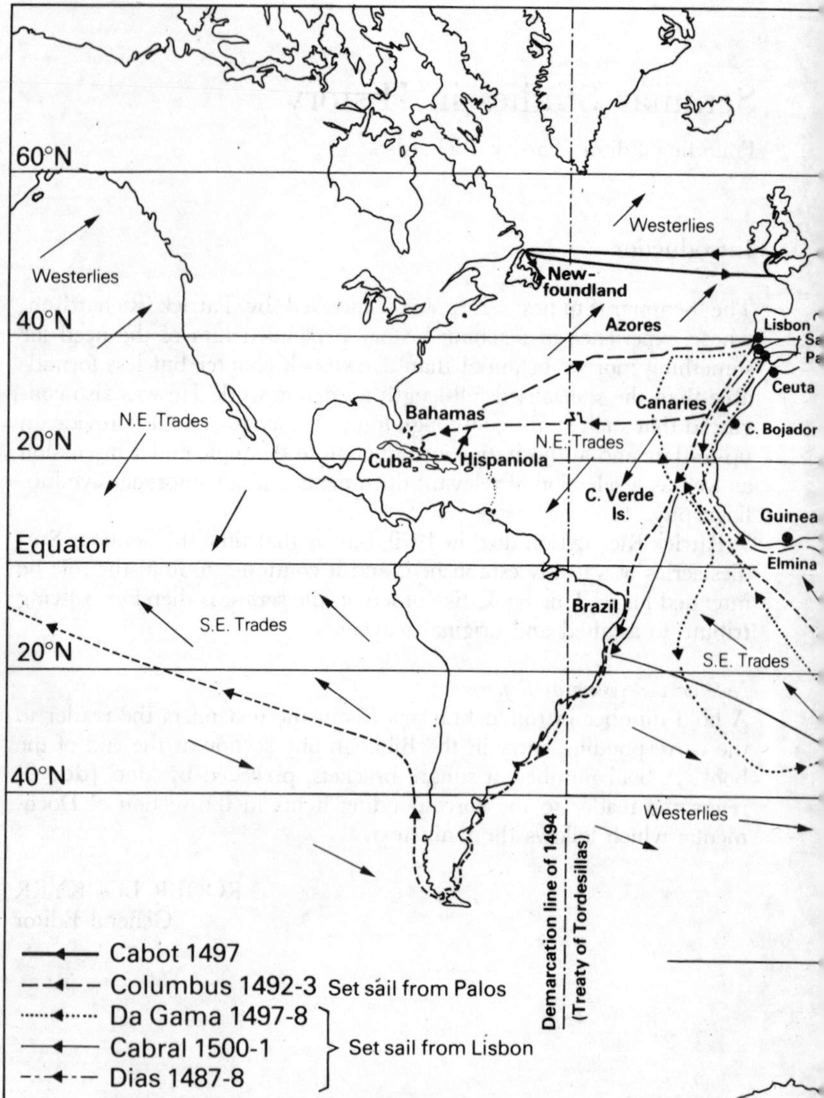
60°N
40°N
20°N
Equator
20°N
40°N
Westerlies
N.E. Trades
S.E. Trades
Westerlies
New-
foundland
Azores
Lisbon
Sa
Pa
Ceuta
Canaries
C. Bojador
Bahamas
Cuba
Hispaniola
N.E. Trades
C. Verde
Is.
Guinea
Elmina
Brazil
S.E. Trades
Westerlies
Demarcation line of 1494
(Treaty of Tordesillas)
Cabot 1497
Columbus 1492-3 Set sail from Palos
Da Gama 1497-8
Cabral 1500-1
Dias 1487-8
Set sail from Lisbon
Magellan/Del Cano 1519-22 Set sail from near Cadiz

The voyages of discovery

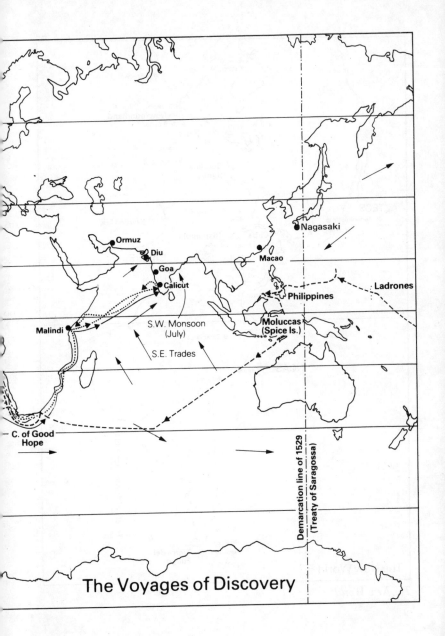

The Voyages of Discovery

Ormuz
Diu
Goa
Calicut
Malindi
Nagasaki
Macao
Philippines
Ladrones
Moluccas (Spice Is.)
S.W. Monsoon (July)
S.E. Trades
C. of Good Hope
Demarcation line of 1529 (Treaty of Saragossa)

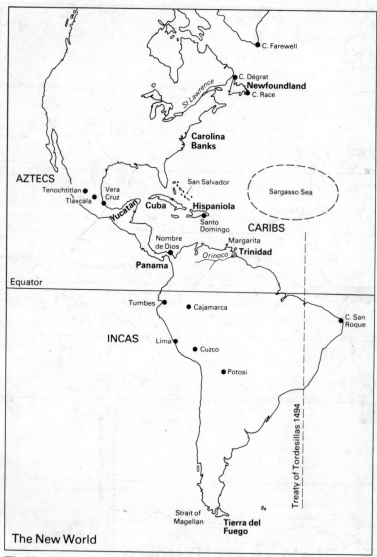

The New World

The New World

Part One: The Background

1 Medieval Europe

The theme of this book is the sensationally rapid opening up of the world by European explorers in the fifteenth and early sixteenth centuries. In 1400 Europe was a largely self-contained region, cut off from other continents and civilizations. By 1550 most of the world's coastlines had been mapped, the Portuguese had built up a trading empire in the Far East and the Spanish ruled vast tracts of America. A linking-up of civilizations had occurred and the world was no longer divided into discrete cultural units separated by wastes of unexplored ocean or desert.

All this was achieved by seamen from a Europe which, in the late fourteenth century, constituted only some 15 per cent of total world population (**30**). The discoveries were not made by Hindus, Arabs or Chinese, although in many respects these peoples were more advanced than Europeans. China, for instance, with a population perhaps double that of Catholic Europe, had an initial lead in the two essential technologies of ship-building and navigation. The white strangers who had visited Calicut a few years before the arrival of Vasco da Gama, and whom the latter believed to be German, were almost certainly Chinese [**doc. 12**]. But China's ancient and sophisticated culture lacked the Westerners' ruthless energy, that unique blend of commercial and religious motivation and sheer will-to-conquer. It was the Portuguese who rounded the Cape of Good Hope and eventually arrived on the door-step of China and not *vice versa*.

The Europe of 1400 was not entirely isolated from the rest of the world. Spices and silks came from the East, via the ports of the Levant or the Black Sea, there to be picked up by Venetian galleys. Along the North African coast gold dust could be obtained, or the inferior pepper known as grains of paradise. However, the rise of the Ottoman Empire during the fourteenth century had severely curtailed these traditional trades, interposing a barrier between Europe and the Far East. In 1256 Marco Polo had set off for China, where he spent fourteen years at the court of the Mongol emperor, Kublai Khan. But those days of relatively facile communication between Europe and Asia were over. The dissolution of the Mongol Empire together with the Ottoman presence had made the land-route to China impassable. During the fifteenth century the advance of the Ottomans was to continue. They came to dominate both the Balkans and the eastern Mediterranean, engulfing the remains of the Byzantine Empire and taking Constantinople in 1453. In the sixteenth century they advanced along the Danube and even threatened Vienna. Thus, paradoxically, at the very moment when the discoveries were opening new windows, Christian Europe itself was contracting.

The discoveries and the Renaissance

The discoveries coincide in time with the Renaissance. Columbus, da Gama and Magellan were the contemporaries of Leonardo, Erasmus and Machiavelli. The two movements have naturally been linked together by historians, for instance in Michelet's definition of the Renaissance as 'the discovery of the world of man'.However, the links connecting them are not easy to establish. The discoverers, on the whole, were practical men, with only a limited interest in the world of Renaissance scholarship. And for most humanists the re-discovery of the ancient world was far more important than the discovery of the new. They felt that the civilizations of Greece and Rome had more to offer than, say, the savagery of Brazil. Another major difference between the two is geographical. The Renaissance was centred in Italy and Burgundy whereas the voyagers set off from Portugal or Spain and latterly from England and France.

Nevertheless it is possible to pick out certain specifically Renaissance characteristics of the discoveries. One is that fifteenth-century explorers were aware of themselves as playing a part in an evolving historical process of discovery. This distinguishes them from their medieval predecessors. Marco Polo was concerned merely to fascinate the reader, to tell anecdotes and recount marvels. The mid-fifteenth-century voyager, Cadamosto, on the other hand, explains that he wrote a journal of his travels 'in order that those that come after me may be able to understand what my thoughts were in the midst of varied things in strange new places'. A century later Chancellor sounds the same note; he writes so that he 'may encourage others to the like travel' (**80**).

A second characteristic is the appetite for fame. It may be true that we usually know little about the personal motivation of the discoverers, but from what we can glean it often seems that, for a

Columbus or a Cortés, the desire for fame was more pronounced than either Christian missionary zeal or even the search for gold. This determination to emulate the heroes of legend and chivalry and to be remembered after their death was one fully shared by Benvenuto Cellini or the artistic contemporaries of Vasari. For this reason *The Lusiads*, the great Portuguese epic poem, is a most fitting monument to Vasco da Gama and his precursors [**doc. 18**] (**6**).

A third Renaissance characteristic is that the discoverers were behaving like scientists, in that they were engaged in an effort to convert cosmographical theory into practice. The voyages of discovery were in a way large-scale experiments, proving or disproving the Renaissance concepts inherited from the ancient world. As J. R. Hale puts it, 'The first scientific laboratory was the world itself' (**80**).

One ought not to exaggerate here. The partnership between theory and discovery was often remote or confused. The discoverers were not open-minded; inevitably they saw through a haze of presuppositions inherited from their Christian beliefs or their read-ings in medieval travel literature. And such presuppositions took centuries to die out. Long after the Portuguese had proved that the Green Sea of Darkness was a myth and the equator not an impen-etrable barrier, Magellan still believed in his Patagonian giants [**doc. 35**], and Cartier in the fabulous kingdom of Saguenay, with its gold, rubies and one-legged pigmies [**doc. 39**].

New demands

Four preconditions were necessary before the discoveries could take place. One was the growth of wealth and an accompanying rise in the demand for certain commodities which Europe could not adequately supply. The second was the development of the skill of map-making, which itself depended in turn on the optimistic view that the world was, in principle, explorable. The third was progress in navigational techniques, and the fourth in ships, sails and naval guns.

By the early fifteenth century Europe had started to recover from the demographic catastrophe of the Black Death. Populations were everywhere on the increase, although still below pre-1349 levels. In the richer parts of Europe – Italy, South Germany, the Netherlands – the tools of commercial capitalism were undergoing rapid devel-opment. As well as great international banks, such as the Fuggers of Augsburg and the Medici of Florence, many lesser concerns now provided facilities for the loan, deposit and exchange of capital. It has been argued that these financial institutions were even more indispensable for setting up the voyages of discovery than the technology of caravels, compasses and quadrants (**30**). Columbus could not have set off on his first voyage if an international consortium of Castilian and Genoese merchants had not put up the capital.

Europe's commercial and financial system was based on a secure supply of precious metal. Between 1000 and 1350 population had increased four-fold and trade perhaps ten-fold but the supply of gold and silver had not kept up. The ensuing money-famine was aggravated by the long-standing deficit in the balance of trade between the Mediterranean region and the East. By 1400, it is true, silver was being mined in Bohemia in large quantities, but gold remained in very short supply. Africa was the world's chief supplier before the discovery of America, but African gold had to be expensively acquired from Moorish traders along the North African coast, rather than from its source south of the Sahara. The demand for gold was thus a major motive for the early voyages.

Another commodity in demand owing to Europe's increasing prosperity was spices. Medieval farmers had always needed to slaughter numbers of beasts in the autumn due to the scarcity of winter fodder. But fifteenth-century accounts show a great increase in meat consumption throughout Europe. This meat was generally of poor quality and could only be preserved and made palatable with large quantities of spices. Preservative spices from the East – Indian pepper, Ceylonese cinnamon, East Indian nutmeg, mace and cloves – traditionally went to the rich man's table. There was now an increasing demand not only for them but for cheaper substitutes such as grains of paradise (Malagueta pepper) from Guinea.

A third commodity which was welcomed by the developing European economies, especially those of Spain and Portugal, was slaves. Since the Black Death there had been an unfulfilled demand for labour. Africa was to provide a reserve which could be drawn upon freely. Occasionally there may have been qualms about the inevitable cruelties of slave traffic [**doc. 5**], but mostly it was argued that the enslavement of pagans was a necessary first step towards their conversion to Christianity. Portugal, in particular, with her population of less than a million, and the increasing demands of her seaborne empire, needed slaves. By the end of the fifteenth century they made up 10 per cent of the population of Lisbon (**30**). Slaves were also used in the Atlantic islands and later

by the Spaniards in America when the Indian population had been
decimated. Long after Africa had run out of gold she could still
supply manpower.

Cosmology

These demands for gold, spices and slaves were functions of a
developing economy, and the incentive to fulfil them provided fuel
for the discoveries. The second precondition was that contemporaries should be open to at least the possibility of trans-continental
voyaging. This had by no means always been the case. It is true
that educated opinion during the Middle Ages believed that the
world was round. Aristotle had proved it from the circular shadow
cast by the earth on the moon during an eclipse, and Plato agreed
with him. Medieval philosophers also referred to the text in Isaiah,
'It is he [God] that sitteth upon the circle of the earth' (**51**). Belief
in a spherical earth as the centre of the universe was an essential
part of the cosmology taught in universities. But to set against such
possibilities, medieval geography had its pessimistic side, which
tended to predominate. Although the earth was round, there was
considerable disagreement about what lay on the other side of it.
There were the spurious, but highly popular, travellers' tales of Sir
John Mandeville and others, with their headless beings and ants the
size of goats [**doc. 2**]. There was, too, the belief, inherited from the
Arabs, that the Atlantic was unnavigable, together with the view of
Pliny that the equator constituted an impassable barrier and that
crews attempting to cross it would be scorched to death. And if land
did exist south of the equator, could it possibly be inhabited? To
believe this, St Augustine had argued, was heresy, since it contra-
dicted the known descent of all mankind from Noah, and in any
case how would the Gospel have been promised to all if these
'Antipodeans' were cut off from Christendom? (**15**)

Ptolemy and Strabo

However, in 1406 there occurred a milestone in Renaissance scholarship, the translation into Latin of Claudius Ptolemy's *Geography*
(**30**). Ptolemy was a Greek of the second century AD, whose
Almagest (Astronomy) had much influenced medieval cosmology.
By the fifteenth century classical authors were acquiring the authority of Holy Writ and this new work attracted enormous attention, becoming the basis of a new school of geography.

5

Ptolemy had made important errors. He postulated a vast southern continent which surrounded the Indian Ocean, thus making India inaccessible by sea. He followed Pliny in saying that the whole southern hemisphere was too hot for human existence. His biggest mistake, however, was to estimate the length of the Eurasian land mass, from Cape St Vincent to the coast of China, as 177 degrees at the equator, instead of the correct figure of 131 degrees. But this turned out to be a fortunate mistake as it encouraged navigators like Columbus and Cabot to try and cross the Atlantic. Ptolemy's major advance was to set out a system of geographical co-ordinates by which the position of any point on the earth's surface could theoretically be described by two figures, its latitude and longitude. This meant – even more theoretically – that it could be reached from any other point, with the aid of a compass and some geometry. Compasses were already in common use, and had been available in the Mediterranean region since the eleventh century. The Ptolemaic maps which accompanied the *Geography* were early exercises in the representation of a curved surface on a flat plane. They showed a European–Asiatic land mass bounded by ocean which was, by implication, navigable, although its full extent was not shown on the maps. The general effect of the *Geography* was to create interest and speculation about the world and the possibilities of its exploration.

Another ancient geographer whose work became known to Europe in the fifteenth century was Strabo, born about 63 BC. Extracts from his works were translated from Greek into Latin and printed in about 1469, but his views were probably known to Italian humanists considerably earlier (**79**). Strabo was more optimistic even than Ptolemy about the possibility of a sea-route to Asia. He wrote, 'The inhabited world forms a complete circle, itself meeting itself; so that, if the immensity of the Atlantic Sea did not prevent, we could sail from Iberia to India along one and the same parallel over the remainder of the circle' (**80**). His views were current among the group of Florentine humanists associated with Cosimo de Medici, one of whom was Paolo Toscanelli. Toscanelli is an important link between early humanism and the discoveries. When he was about 76, he wrote his famous letter to Columbus of 1474 which encouraged the latter to sail westwards [**doc. 20**]. The really important new concept derived from Ptolemy and Strabo, and held by humanists such as Toscanelli, was that the ocean, instead of being a barrier, could be a waterway. This was the main geographical idea that broke through the strait-jacket of medieval thought.

There was always, however, a considerable gap between academic geography and the contemporary experience of practical seamen. The latter certainly had the aid of charts when they sailed in known waters but late medieval portolan charts were based on years of experience and owed little to theoretical studies. They consisted of clear and accurate coastal outlines and were criss-crossed by networks of rhumb lines emanating from strategically placed compass roses. Portolans were not drawn to a consistent projection, however, and so were accurate only for short passages. Not until the sixteenth century did Mercator produce his famous projection on which both latitude and longitude could be shown by straight lines (**33**).

Navigation

As far as fifteenth-century navigational techniques were concerned, there was again a gap between academics and seamen. For problems of astronomy and astrology medieval scholars possessed the astrolabe, an instrument of great beauty and complexity, but not at all suitable for the deck of a heaving ship. In fact, early fifteenth-century seamen probably did not use the heavens at all for navigation. They relied on the old technique of dead reckoning, whereby a daily estimate of the ship's position was pricked on to the chart, after the length, speed and direction of its course during that day had all been allowed for. The first recorded use of the stars, a measurement of the angle of elevation of the Pole Star to estimate latitude, was in 1462, two years after the death of Prince Henry (**60, 93**).

An even more significant date was 1484, when there took place a major step in bringing together academic science and practical skills. That year a group of astronomers consulted by John II of Portugal suggested that a ship's latitude might be best calculated from the height of the midday sun. This was easier to measure than that of the fairly faint Pole Star, especially as the Pole Star tended to dip towards the horizon the nearer voyagers approached the equator in their exploration of the West African coast [**doc. 8**]. To convert the angle of the sun's elevation into the observer's latitude required a set of tables of the sun's declination, that is, of the position of the sun as seen by an observer at the equator, at any given day of the year. Such tables had been compiled in 1478 by Abraham Zacuto, a Portuguese Jew who became Astronomer Royal in Lisbon. With their aid it was comparatively easy to calculate latitude by readings from a quadrant, or an astrolabe modified for sea use. This was a revolutionary advance. It meant that Vasco da Gama and Cabral could practise the modified dead reckoning technique known as running down one's latitude, which involved sailing north or south until astronomical observations showed that the correct latitude had been reached, and then proceeding east or west along it until one made the desired landfall.

This relatively oblique method of approaching one's goal was made necessary because no one at that time had evolved a satisfactory way of estimating longitude from on board ship, a problem whose solution had to wait until the appearance of an accurate chronometer, in Captain Cook's day. Nevertheless, by the beginning of the sixteenth century celestial navigation was beginning to be part of the standard training of ships' officers, as is borne out by the instructions given to Amerigo Vespucci on his appointment as Chief Pilot of Spain in 1508 [**doc. 25**]. To sum up, the early fifteenth-century voyagers used a conservative navigational techinique, but from the 1480s astronomical navigation played an increasingly important role and without it the Portuguese achievement in the Far East would scarcely have been possible.

Ships and sails

The importance of the evolution of a suitable ship as a precondition for the discoveries is obvious. By 1400 nations bordering on the Atlantic had numbers of ocean-going sailing ships, although in the Mediterranean oared galleys continued to predominate until the end of the sixteenth century. These Atlantic ships, known as cobs, were heavy, broad, tub-like and clinker-built – that is, of overlapping wooden beams. Their clumsiness was accentuated by square rigging, which made it impossible for them to sail at all close to the wind. The advantage of square rig was that a large area of canvas could be carried with safety, as the various sails could be handled separately in a gale, and also it was effective given a following wind. But the cob, while serviceable for general trading, was unsuitable for exploration, which might involve negotiating unfamiliar coastlines with shoals and estuaries and unknown currents and winds (**64**).

It was therefore of key significance that another tradition of shipbuilding was available to the Portuguese in the early fifteenth century. It was that of the caravel, a slimmer, lighter ship, lower in water, with lateen rigging rather than square. This tradition derived from the Arabs, and the Portuguese probably encountered it in the course of their long struggle against the Moors of North Africa. The caravel's triangular lateen sail, bent on a long yard hoisted obliquely to the mast, has been called the special contribution of Arab civilization to Western technology and as characteristic of Islam as the crescent itself (**56**). Lateen rigging allowed a ship to sail much closer to the wind and to make way under a lighter breeze than did square rigging.

The caravels which Prince Henry sent out from Sagres were thus different in rig and design from the cobs of northern Europe, although their methods of construction were similar – they were clinker-built rather than caravel-built, as were Arab ships. During the century Portuguese ship-building evolved considerably, and the two traditions were further successfully combined in the *caravela redonda*, a three-masted caravel with a flexible combination of lateen and square rigging. Most of the ships of the late fifteenth and sixteenth-century voyages were of this pattern. They were usually very small. John Cabot reached Newfoundland in 1497 in a ship of 50 tonnes, with a crew of 18 or 20; Columbus's three ships in 1492 had a total complement of 90; Magellan set off round the world with five ships of 470 tonnes in all. And this was at a time when merchant ships of 1,000 tonnes were by no means rare. Furthermore, the ships of the discoverers must have been extremely uncomfortable to serve in. There was no special provision for sleeping accommodation, except for senior officers, and very little in the way of cooking or sanitary facilities. Foul water, scurvy and rats were normal accompaniments to any long voyage (**54**).

It is clear, however, that the caravel was very suitable for its role. It was fast, manoeuvrable and durable. And it had another advantage which became plain when hostile maritime powers were met with in the Indian Ocean – it made an excellent fighting unit. The Portuguese were the first to recognize the gun rather than the foot soldier as the most effective weapon in naval warfare. Early fifteenth-century caravels had small guns mounted fore and aft, but by the end of the century the guns had become larger, and embrasures were cut in the gunwales through which broadsides could be fired. The spectacular victory of Diu, in 1509, over a combined Egyptian and Gujurati fleet, proved the supremacy of Portuguese naval gunnery over all comers.

Part Two: Descriptive Analysis

2 Portugal

One obvious question relating to the discoveries is how they came to be initiated by Portugal, a small, poor and culturally backward country on the fringe of western Europe. In the early fifteenth century Portugal's population was less than a million. There was only one university, of a low academic status, which fluctuated between Lisbon and Coimbra. Of the few towns of any importance, Lisbon, easily the largest, had about 40,000 people. The Portuguese commercial middle class was tiny and mainly confined to Lisbon and Oporto, where it tended to be dominated by foreign communities of merchants such as the Venetians and Genoese. The mass of the population were peasants, subsisting often on inferior soils. In the north, land holdings were small, and the province of Minho, especially, was overcrowded. In the southern provinces of Alentejo and the Algarve, more recently seized from the Moors, there were larger estates, together with a class of landless labourers. The Portuguese nobility, led by the royal House of Avis, were a warlike, impetuous and superstitious class, permeated by late medieval chivalric values and comparatively untouched by the Renaissance. Yet it was this rather insignificant nation which, in less than a century, changed the map of the world by discovering the entire coastline of Africa – a continent hitherto practically unknown to Christian Europe – and penetrating to India and the Far East (**56, 60**).

One clear advantage possessed by Portugal was her geographical position. Not only did she have several hundred kilometres of Atlantic coastline (though few good natural harbours), but also the coast was well positioned for favourable winds and currents to Africa. Her great rival, Castile, on the other hand, looked more towards the Mediterranean, especially after the link with Aragon was established through the marriage of Ferdinand and Isabella in 1469.

Another advantage Portugal had over Castile was that she was already, by the thirteenth century, a unified nation. The last Moors had been expelled in 1249, over two centuries before the Castilian conquest of Granada. And a further, though less tangible, factor was the character of the Portuguese nobility themselves, the class that was to provide the leadership for the voyages. The earliest voyages of discovery had very little commercial significance. They were essentially daring ventures into the unknown, tempered with a strong and aggressive crusading impulse. Not until the voyages organised by Fernão Gomes, and the building of the trading base at Elmina in 1481, did clear commercial prospects start to emerge [**docs. 9, 10**]. Before this time there was little to attract the great Italian merchants and bankers, who sought less risky ventures in which to invest their capital. The early challenge needed a less materialistic and more reckless response (**56**).

Prince Henry

The battle of Aljubarrota in 1385 ended a war between Castile and Portugal in the latter's favour, and brought to the Portuguese throne the House of Avis, in the person of John I. The Portuguese had won with the assistance of English bowmen and to cement this alliance John married Philippa, daughter of John of Gaunt. The third surviving child of this marriage was Prince Henry, born in 1394, who is said to have initiated the Portuguese voyages of exploration after he became governor of the Algarve in 1419. Unfortunately, little is known today about the prince; the main, and almost the sole, source for his life is the contemporary chronicle of Azurara (**2**). This has not prevented a vast corpus of historical writing about him, much of it apocryphal. He was nicknamed 'the Navigator' by a nineteenth-century English biographer, yet he never travelled farther than Tangier. It has also been said that he maintained a school of navigational and geographical lore at Sagres in the Algarve; that he himself was a Renaissance scholar; that he planned to reach India. Probably none of this is true; however, he did provide an important stimulus and patronage for many, though far from all, of the voyages made between 1419 and his death in 1460. It was partly to win honour in his eyes that the Portuguese captains strove to excel each other (**35, 60, 68**).

Henry's primary motives were neither scientific nor commercial, though it is true that he may have heard about the gold dust which caravans brought to Ceuta from south of the Sahara. Portugal was particularly short of this commodity, being one of the few European nations without a gold coinage. There is no need to distrust the list of motives which Azurara ascribes to Henry [**doc. 3**], a mixture of religious, strategic and even astrological – the need to fulfil the predictions of his horoscope. The planning and financing of the early voyages by Henry has been described as an early example of state-capitalistic enterprise (**30**), but contemporaries probably saw it as more like a living extension of the Arthurian legend, with Prester John substituted for the Holy Grail, and caravels for chargers.

The fall of Ceuta in 1415 starts the saga of Portuguese exploration. Ceuta, on the North African coast almost opposite Gibraltar, was an important Moslem port and the terminal point of various caravan routes. Azurara explains how the four sons of King John begged their father to undertake some great crusading venture so that they might earn their knighthoods in battle. John was anxious to employ the thousands of soldiers idle since the end of the war against Castile, and a major expedition involving over 200 vessels was mounted. The story of the capture of this stronghold and its retention against fierce counter-attack is a stirring one (**60**). Its acquisition by Portugal burst the geographical boundaries of medieval Europe and it is likely that in Ceuta the Portuguese learnt at first hand about the geography of north-west Africa. Its conquest reduced the danger of Moroccan intervention when the exploration of the Atlantic coast of Africa started and also, because of the weakening of Morocco's trade links with Africa south of the Sahara, made it even more necessary for Portugal to establish her own direct sea communication with Guinea, from where the gold ultimately came.

Having been rewarded by John for his valour at Ceuta with the governorship of the Algarve, Henry turned his attention to further southward penetration. In about 1419, ships dispatched by him from Sagres reached the islands of Porto Santo and Madeira, which the Portuguese proceeded to colonise and exploit with the introduction of sugar cane and grapes. In 1421, if not earlier, he started to send out annual voyages to explore the Atlantic coast of West Africa. Until then the limit of exploration had been Cape Non, or 'No', beyond which, it was thought, lay the torrid zone where, if a white man entered, the heat would turn him black and scorch him to death (**60**).

A few hundred kilometres to the south of Cape Non was another obstacle, Cape Bojador, where the sea was treacherously shallow for several kilometres out from the coast, and the currents rapid. It needed all Henry's powers of persuasion before one of his captains, Gil Eannes, finally passed this point, in 1434 [**doc. 4**]. These successes were milestones in the history of human achievement.

Greater than the physical dangers must have been the psychological barriers behind which lay the totally unknown, peopled perhaps with the monsters of Mandeville, or worse.

Henry was a man of many parts. Much of his time was spent at court as adviser to successive monarchs, and he was also master of the important chivalric Order of Christ, a post which gave him access to great wealth but was also demanding of his time. It is likely that he rarely lived at Sagres where legend has him presiding over his nautical academy, though he may have stayed sometimes at neighbouring Lagos, from which he received a share of the customs revenues.

In 1437 the voyages were halted when Henry became involved in a disastrous expedition to Tangier in which he and his whole army had to surrender to the Moors, and he was forced to leave his youngest brother, Ferdinand, a hostage in their hands. Shortly after this, Henry's brother, King Duarte, died leaving a son of six, and as a result yet another brother, Pedro, became regent. From 1440 until his death in civil war in 1449 it was the much-travelled and cultured Pedro, rather than Henry, who provided the main initiative for discovery (**68**).

By this time the Azores had been discovered, probably accidentally by ships returning from West Africa and standing out to sea in order to cut across the north-easterly winds. Their date of first sighting is uncertain, but a chart of 1435 has certain islands in the right position with the legend 'newly found islands' (**34**).

By Henry's death, in 1460, the African coast had been explored and charted down to Sierra Leone at about latitude 8 degrees north, although some authorities think that Cape Palmas, some 960 kilometres further on, had been reached (**35, 60**). The names of many Portuguese captains, known from the pages of Azurara, are linked to this achievement. But the best documented voyages of this period were those made by the Venetian, Cadamosto. This young adventurer was travelling from the Mediterranean to Holland when bad weather drove his ship into Sagres harbour and he met Prince Henry. Cadamosto was so impressed with the latest news about the riches and opportunities of the African project that he volunteered to undertake a voyage for Henry, who was to provide and provision a caravel and receive half of any proceeds. Luckily for us Cadamosto was a keen observer of anthropological and botanical detail who compiled his own chronicle [**doc. 6**] (**8**). His first voyage, in 1455, took him, via Madeira and the Canaries, to the island of Arguim near Cape Branco, where the Portuguese had just built a trading station. This was not only the first Portuguese base of a chain which was to stretch to Macão, but it was also the first of all the European colonial forts and factories shortly to encircle the entire globe. The next year Cadamosto again sailed to Africa and saw elephants and horse-fishes (hippopotamuses). On this occasion he noted that the North Star, used by navigators when trying to fix their latitude, was fast disappearing below the horizon, but that another constellation, the Southern Cross, had appeared as a substitute [**doc. 7**].

During the year of Cadamosto's first voyage Henry had secured his new lands and gained a diplomatic achievement by obtaining from Pope Nicholas V a Bull, *Pontifex Romanus*, which recognised Portugal's monopoly of African discoveries. The Bull described as belonging to Portugal the entire coastline 'extending from Cape Bojador and Cape Non through all Guinea and passing beyond to the southern parts', and threatened those who interfered with this monopoly with the penalty of excommunication (**34**).

After Henry's death Portuguese energies and finance were again diverted into attacks on the coastal towns of Morocco, and the only maritime achievement over the next few years was the discovery of the Cape Verde Islands. In 1470 Alfonso V succeeded to the throne. He again was not primarily interested in exploration, but he did lease the monopoly of West African trade to a wealthy Lisbon merchant, Fernão Gomes, on condition that a hundred leagues of coastline a year be explored, starting at Sierra Leone [**doc. 9**]. No chronicles of the voyages made under this contract have survived, but they were apparently successful, as Gomes's captains traversed extensively southwards along the coasts of present-day Ghana, Nigeria and the Cameroons. Undoubtedly by this time the route to India had become a major motive for further exploration. This is proved by certain connections which have come to light between the Portuguese Crown and Italian geographers. In 1459 the celebrated Venetian map-maker, Fra Mauro, dispatched a map of the world to the King of Portugal (**33**). Also the Florentine humanist, Paolo Toscanelli, had written to the King advising him on the quickest route to Asia (which he believed to be across the Atlantic and not round Africa) [**doc. 20**]. This letter was written 'before the wars in Castile', i.e. before 1464. The eastward trend of the African coast must have given rise to hopes – soon to be disappointed by a new change of direction southwards – that the way to the Indian Ocean lay open.

Nearly 3,200 kilometres of coastline were explored during Gomes's contract but he did not seek to renew it in 1475, perhaps because of the increased costs and dangers to trade after the renewed outbreak of war with Castile. This was the War of Succession, between Alfonso, who supported the claim of his wife and niece, Joanna, to the throne of Castile, and Isabella, backed by her father-in-law, John II of Aragon. It involved four years of bitter fighting, not only on the Spanish mainland but also in the various Atlantic islands and along the Guinea coast. Although Alfonso lost the war and had to acknowledge Isabella as Queen of Castile, the Portuguese held their own at sea. The Treaty of Alcaçovas, in 1479, gave Portugal monopoly rights in the Guinea trade, and ownership over three of the four island groups under dispute. Castile gained only the Canaries; the Cape Verde islands, Madeira and the Azores remained Portuguese.

Cão and Dias

In 1481 the capable monarch, John II, succeeded to the throne and a more energetic maritime policy was initiated. The fort at Arguim was strengthened and a new and larger one built at Elmina, where a profitable trade in gold dust, slaves, malagueta pepper, and other, more exotic commodities such as ostrich eggs soon developed [**doc. 10**]. Immediately following this came the two voyages of Diego Cão, one of the most successful of all the Portuguese explorers; his successor was Bartholemew Dias, who rounded the Cape of Good Hope.

By now navigational methods had improved, and Cão was probably the first explorer regularly to use a nautical almanac which allowed latitudes to be easily calculated from quadrant readings of the angle of the North Star or the Southern Cross (**68**). On his first voyage, in 1482, he explored a long stretch of coast, from the equator to Cape Cross in present-day South-West Africa (Namibia). On his second he sailed up the estuary of the River Congo and made contact with the king of that region. Again, records of these voyages have vanished, although they are described by sixteenth-century chroniclers such as Barros (**5**). The Portuguese policy of secrecy, which involved giving away as little information to other nations as possible, may have had something to do with the general lack of maps and documentation from which we suffer today. There has been debate among historians as to the extent of this censorship, but there is little doubt of its existence (**33, 49**). There is internal evidence that even chronicles which have come down to us, such as those by Azurara (**2**) and Pacheo (**21**) have been extensively tampered with. John II and Manuel of Portugal decreed the death penalty for those caught smuggling charts out of the country. In view of this shortage of documentary material, one primary source which becomes all the more important in the case of Cão, and also of Dias, is the limestone pillars, or padroes, which these explorers took with them from Lisbon and erected at prominent places during their voyages. One of the most enthralling episodes in the historiography of the discoveries is the account of the South African historian, Eric Axelson, of how he sought out the precise location of several of these pillars, including both the last one erected by Cão at Cape Cross (latitude 21 degrees south) and Dias's furthest one at Mossel Bay, east of the Cape of Good Hope (**27**). The inscriptions on these pillars, where they have survived, have provided vital clues for reconstructing the chronology of the voyages [**doc. 11**].

Cão's voyages proved how inhospitable the coasts of Angola and Namibia were. Water could be found here and there, but food was a major problem in these unpopulated regions. Dias therefore took, in addition to his two caravels, a store ship which he left at Walvis Bay. He beat southwards against wind and current, then stood out to sea in the neighbourhood of Cape Volta, having picked up the prevailing Westerlies, and eventually ran east and doubled the Cape of Good Hope without sighting it. He coasted on as far as the Great Fish River. There, although he must have realised from the warm current as well as the trend of the coast that the way to India lay open at last, he was persuaded to turn back by his crew who feared for their food supplies. On the return journey they sighted the Cape which they had previously missed. Dias named it the Cape of Storms, but King John changed the name to the Cape of Good Hope because it promised the way to India. The store ship was located, nine months after he had left it, but with only three of its crew left alive, and in December 1488, after having been away for over 16 months, Dias returned home. He had made a greater contribution to the discovery of the route to the East than any other individual. Not only had he rounded the Cape but also he had, perhaps by chance, discovered the best method of rounding it, on a wide seaward tack (**43**).

Before Dias's return, John II had dispatched Pedro de Covilhã, whose mission was, travelling by the land-route, to discover what he could about India, and also to contact Prester John. This mythical Christian monarch, whose kingdom was popularly supposed to exist somewhere in the heart of pagan Africa, or possibly Asia, was still thought of by the Portuguese at this date as a potential ally against the Moslems. During the late Middle Ages belief in his existence had formed an important part of the mythology of a beleaguered Christendom although the first reference to him in Western literature occurs as early as 1145 (**43, 81**). Covilhã was a suitable choice for this hazardous mission. He had served the monarchs of both Spain and Portugal, latterly as a spy, and he spoke Arabic. John's cosmographers primed him with the latest geographical information, and he set off with a companion in May 1487. They travelled via Italy and Rhodes to·Alexandria, where both nearly died of fever. From there, Covilhã alone made his way to Aden and then in an Arab dhow to Calicut, the richest port in India. After numerous adventures the found himself back in Egypt about four years after first leaving Portugal. Somewhat naturally he wanted to go home, but received a message from two Jews sent by John that he must on no account do so before finding Prester John. Covilhã then sent a report home full of useful information about India and the route to it. It is likely, but not certain, that this information was available to Vasco da Gama before he set out in 1497. Covilhã's adventures meanwhile continued, and their climax was a visit to holy Mecca disguised as a Moslem pilgrim – probably the first time a Christian had dared such a feat. Finally he reached Abyssinia, whose king, a Coptic Christian, appeared to be the contemporary ruler who came nearest to the image of Prester John. Covilhã spent the rest of his life, some 30 years, either as a prisoner or as a guest of this monarch.

The ten-year gap between the return of Dias and the dispatch of da Gama to India in 1497 needs some explanation, and there are several factors which may help to account for it. In the first place, Covilhã's report may have arrived in the mid-1490s, requiring analysis and assimilation by the royal experts. However, some of the mistakes da Gama made when in India, and in particular his assumption that the Hindus were some kind of Christian [**doc. 16**], as well as his gross underestimate of the kind of gift suitable for an Indian ruler [**doc. 15**], would surely have been obviated by the information from Covilhã. It is therefore possible that Covilhã's report did not arrive before da Gama's departure. Secondly, Columbus's return from Hispaniola in 1493, after his first voyage, complicated the diplomatic scene. Columbus landed at Lisbon and met John, apparently receiving a polite reception before he proceeded to Spain. The Portuguese King, primed by the same experts as had been sceptical about Columbus's project in the first place, may not have believed his claim to have reached Asia, but in any case there was a clear need for negotiations between Spain and Portugal as to their respective rights in the newly explored areas. The Pope also entered these negotiations by virtue of his recognised authority to allot sovereignty over any lands not already possessed by a Christian prince. Alexander VI was a Spaniard who owed a favour to Ferdinand and Isabella, not least because he was enjoying the fruits of three Aragonese bishoprics. He therefore published a series of Bulls highly favourable to Spain which cancelled earlier papal grants to Portugal such as those acquired by Prince Henry in 1455. But determined Portuguese bargaining led to the more equitable Treaty of Tordesillas which contained the famous line of demarcation across the Atlantic [**doc. 24**]. This agreement was a diplomatic achievement all round because it meant that the two rivals could each proceed to rapid colonial expansion without friction – something which more recent colonial powers have not usually found possible. All this diplomacy took time, and the year after the treaty John II died, his death no doubt leading to a further delay in dispatching a new expedition to the East.

The final factor causing an apparent delay is that there may well have been, in fact, other Portuguese voyages between 1488 and 1497. There are several pieces of circumstantial evidence leading to this conclusion. First, da Gama's expedition was well prepared, with a planning more suited to an armed trading venture than to a voyage of discovery. There were four ships, and the two largest were square-rigged *nãos*, larger than caravels, and carrying 20 guns between them. Such rigging indicated a confidence that the expedition would find favourable winds, and not have to beat against the wind as both Cão and Dias did down the south-western coast of Africa. Secondly, da Gama himself was not a professional seaman but a nobleman, a suitable choice for a first encounter with unknown foreign dignitaries. And why, it might be asked, was da Gama given such an important command at all if he had never proved himself on previous voyages? Finally, da Gama's course was not the same as those of Cão or Dias. Instead of hugging the African coast he followed a wide sweep out into the western Atlantic, which took him close to the coast of Brazil. This was a course which made the best possible use of prevailing winds, in particular minimising the time and effort spent beating against the South-East Trades (**32, 43**).

All this strongly points to the probability that da Gama knew what he was doing because of information collected on previous voyages. We know nothing about any such voyages. However, Portuguese governmental records show that during this decade large quantities of ship's biscuit were purchased for unspecified purposes (**32**). Furthermore, a twentieth-century Russian historian came across an Arabic reference to Portuguese ships being wrecked on the shoals of Sofala, a port in East Africa, apparently prior to da Gama's voyage. The Portuguese policy of secrecy may account for the absence of any further evidence (**34, 35, 76**).

Vasco da Gama

Vasco da Gama's first voyage is rightly among the most famous of all the voyages in history (**35, 43, 60**). The story fascinates because it involves an early encounter, not to say clash, between two civilizations. India was represented by the urbane and tolerant Hindu ruler of Calicut, the Samorin, reclining, when da Gama first saw him, on a green velvet couch and holding a golden spittoon [**doc. 13**]. Europe was represented by da Gama and his shabby crew, supremely confident of the superiority of their manners, religion and nation, and always ready to unsheath their daggers at any imagined insult. The contrast was not particularly flattering to the West. Da Gama himself was a ruthless and cruel leader. On one occasion during his second voyage he captured a shipload of Moslem pilgrims returning from Mecca and set it on fire, burning men, women and children because they refused him a suitable tribute. On another, he caused the severed limbs of a number of innocent fishermen to be put in a boat to drift shoreward in order to terrify the Samorin of Calicut into complying with his demands [**doc. 17**].

A further aspect of this voyage is that it represents one of the greatest navigational feats of the period. Da Gama was three months out of sight of land on his outward voyage, as compared with Columbus's 33 days between the Canaries and the Bahamas in 1492. Moreover Columbus crossed the Atlantic by keeping more or less to the same line of latitude, whereas da Gama had to exploit a complex wind system and end up at the right point to negotiate the Cape of Good Hope.

Da Gama left Lisbon in July 1497 and early in 1498 made contact with the outposts of Moslem civilization in the ports of East Africa. After a hostile reception at Mombasa he obtained, by a great stroke of luck, the services of a famous Arab navigator named Ibn Mejid, who piloted his squadron across the Indian Ocean to Calicut. This rich port, like others along the Malabar coast of India, was governed by a Hindu prince, but all the commerce was in the hands of Arabs or Indian Moslems who lived in separate communities from the Hindu majority, well treated by the authorities and at peace with their neighbours. Da Gama discovered quickly not only that his appearance was resented by the Calicut Moslems, but also that the presents for the ruler, as well as the goods which he had brought to barter, were highly inferior to what was available locally [**doc. 15**]. Although the Samorin was hospitable and courteous, his officials openly laughed at the washing basins, casks of oil and strings of coral which da Gama had brought. These were presents more appropriate for the headman of an African village. Da Gama had the greatest difficulty in trading at all, but through persistence he eventually collected some pepper and cinnamon and, after a bitter argument about customs dues, left for home, which he reached in September 1499. The voyage had lasted over two years and cost the lives of half his men, but it was epoch-making. The link between Europe and India had finally and permanently been established. According to the Indian historian, K. M. Panikkar, the da Gama epoch of world history had now commenced, an epoch which was to last until 1947, the year of India's independence from Britain (**53**). Pannikar describes the main features of this period as 'the dominance of maritime power over the land masses of Asia; the imposition of a commercial economy over communities whose economic life in the past had not been based on international trade; and thirdly, the domination of the people of Europe, who held the mastery of the seas, over the affairs of Asia'.

So far as the Indian Ocean is concerned, the Portuguese were to achieve this domination within a few years of da Gama's voyage. Two causes of their superiority were their tenacity of purpose and their naval gunnery. A third was that they were fortunate in the timing of their arrival, because no single great maritime power existed in the area to challenge them. The largest Indian state in 1498 was the Hindu kingdom of Vijayanagar, which had no access to the sea. Along the Malabar coast there were many small states which the Portuguese could play off against each other, and the same was true of the East African coast. Egypt and Persia were powerful states, but both were a long way off and did not maintain permanent fleets in the Indian Ocean. Ming China was even more powerful, but the Chinese had reversed their earlier expansionist policy and no longer visited the area (**30**).

Empire

During the five years after da Gama's return in 1499 the Portuguese dispatched every available ship and man to India in a series of voyages starting with Cabral's 13-vessel expedition of 1500. About 7,000 men went out in this five-year period. The experience of da Gama and Cabral showed that the commerce of the Malabar coast would have to be wrested by force from the Moslem merchants who controlled it, and many of the ships sent out were not intended to trade but to remain permanently in Indian waters as warships.

The first viceroy for India, Francisco de Almeida, was dispatched in 1505 and his instructions from King Manuel already show a sophisticated strategy for the creation of a seaborne empire based on the control of certain key ports. Almeida was a ferocious military commander and when his son was killed in 1508 during a skirmish with an Egyptian fleet newly arrived in the Indian Ocean he retaliated the next year by taking on and annihilating the Egyptians and their Gujurati allies in the large harbour of the Hindu port of Diu, to the north of Calicut. The Egyptian commander, Mir Hussain, planned to entice the Portuguese ships inshore, where they would be at the mercy of the Diu land batteries, but Almeida foresaw this manoeuvre and anchored his ships. The carnage brought about by Portuguese naval gunnery was vast and the whole harbour was dyed crimson with enemy blood. It was one of the most decisive sea battles of the time, and permanently established Western superiority throughout the Indian Ocean (**43**). Shortly after the battle, Almeida was recalled to Portugal, but was killed on the way home by a Hottentot assegai.

During the period of office of the next viceroy, Alfonso de Albuquerque (1509–15), the strategic plan outlined to Almeida became reality. In 1510 Goa was captured from the Hindu state of Bijapur. Goa was a significant port with a sizeable population, including a merchant community which could be taxed by the Portuguese, but its main advantage lay in its superb position. It was 8 kilometres up an estuary, and hence out of reach of storms, and it was on an easily defensible island, separated from the mainland by a creek which had been thoughtfully stocked with crocodiles to discourage enemies and runaway slaves. Its possession by the Portuguese proved to Indian rulers that they had come to stay, and could no longer be regarded as a momentarily dangerous set of pirates. As Albuquerque wrote to Manuel: 'The capture of Goa alone worked more to the credit of your Majesty than fifteen-years-worth of armadas that were sent out to India' (**35**).

Goa was the first and most important of a chain of bases which Albuquerque and his successors set up. Another great achievement was the capture of Malacca in 1511. This port was the rich entrepôt between the Pacific and Indian Oceans, and was especially important for the spice trade. Its taking constituted another heroic episode in the same mould as Cortés's capture of Tenochtitlan. An army of 900 Portuguese and 200 Indian mercenaries took on some 30,000 defenders, who also possessed artillery. A ruthless and well-co-ordinated attack was pressed home for several days, the climax being when Portuguese soldiers, who had never before seen an elephant, routed those of the Sultan by fearlessly jabbing them with lances in their tender parts.

In 1513 Albuquerque failed to breach the strong walls of Aden, at the mouth of the Red Sea. Two years later, however, he captured Ormuz on the northern shore of the Persian Gulf. Shortly after this feat Albuquerque received the news of his replacement as viceroy. This illustrates an important weakness in the Portuguese chain of command. Manuel, like other contemporary European monarchs, was afraid of allowing his nobles too much power. Although it was hardly possible, owing to the distance involved, to keep a close watch from Lisbon on the actions of a viceroy in India, Manuel made up for this by making their term of office extremely short, usually three years or less, and by sending out a new viceroy some time before the previous one's term had elapsed, so as to act as a check. Albuquerque might have gone on to expand the network of empire he had built. His plans for the future included an alliance with the Shiite Moslem Persians against the Sunnite Ottomans, together with a more far-fetched scheme to persuade the king of Abyssinia to divert the waters of the Nile into the Red Sea, thus starving Egypt into submission (**43**). Nevertheless he was already 56 when he became viceroy, over-age for such a demanding role. His years in office were crucial in the development of Portuguese power in the East, and he was perhaps the ablest naval strategist of his day, a ruthless and effective leader of men.

Little that Albuquerque had not attempted or anticipated was achieved by his successors. Later viceroys, with the notable exception of João de Castro (1545–8), were a fairly indifferent lot, who failed to hold their unruly subordinates in the discipline to which Albuquerque had subjected them, so that private trading and corruption flourished. Manuel and his successor, John III, starved the empire of men and ships, Manuel in particular diverting much-needed resources to crusading projects in North Africa. During this period the only major territorial gains were Ceylon, on which a fort was built in 1518, and Diu, captured in 1535.

In 1513 a treaty had been made with the Sultan of Ternate, the principal clove-producing island in the East Indies. This allowed the Portuguese to build a fortified warehouse, and Ternate became another base in the network, although they never owned the island and their hold on it was precarious.

The commercial success of the Portuguese was based partly on the exaction of duties on the trade of other nations in areas under their control, and partly on their own diverse and profitable trading. The main commodity imported from the East to Portugal was spices, mainly pepper which came originally from Sumatra, but also cinnamon from Ceylon, camphor from Borneo, nutmeg from the Banda Islands, cloves from the Moluccas, and many others. To pay for these the Portuguese developed a network of ancillary trades. For instance they exported Indian cottons to Indonesia as well as to East Africa, and Arab horses from Mesopotamia to India. In the 1550s a profitable and exotic trade was set up which involved sending an annual carrack – the famous Black Ship – from Goa to carry European goods to the Portuguese base at Macão, where Chinese silks were loaded, to be in turn sold at Nagasaki, mainly in return for silver. The Portuguese were the first world-wide traders, and Portuguese became the *lingua franca* of Asiatic maritime trade.

Decline

By the mid-sixteenth century the Portuguese Empire was still functioning efficiently, and the Portuguese monopoly of sea-borne trade between Europe and the East had not yet been breached by other powers. Their achievement in the East seems more spectacular than the corresponding Spanish conquests in America when one considers, first, that the Portuguese never had a population of more than a million and a quarter; secondly, that they were simultaneously controlling a stretch of the Brazilian coast – first visited by Cabral in 1500 (**13**) – and also maintaining permanent bases in both West and East Africa; thirdly, that the technological gap between the Portuguese and their main Asian rivals was not nearly so great as that between the Spaniards and the subject peoples of America.

However, this vast imperial effort could not last. The most obvious factor in the rapid decline of the empire over the second half of the century was the drain on manpower. Throughout the century an average of 2,400 people a year emigrated from Portugal (**28**). Most of these were young, able-bodied males, and most never returned. Many died during their initial six-to-eight month voyage to India. Many were posted to fever-stricken regions in Africa or Asia, whereas most Spaniards abroad lived in the healthier uplands of Peru or Mexico. One partial solution to this manpower problem was intermarriage with the locals; another was the employment of non-Europeans in the army or navy; both of these solutions ultimately weakened the empire.

Another cause of decline was the ever-increasing demand for ships which Portugal did not have the resources, particularly the timber, to build. There were perhaps 300 ocean-going ships at the height of the empire, an impressive total, but nothing like enough to carry all the goods and police all the trade routes. A tendency to use larger and larger ships on the India route – though without any corresponding improvements in design – was one outcome of this. The *Madre de Dios*, the Portuguese Indiaman taken by an English privateer in 1592, was rated at 1,600 tonnes, and it was reported of her that in a heavy sea it needed 12 or 14 men to control her tiller.

A third factor in the decline was that the uncompromisingly crusading style of the Portuguese tended to isolate them, and prevent the development of friendly commercial or diplomatic relations with non-Christians. Typical of this was the Portuguese attitude to Hindus, once they had progressed beyond da Gama's assumption that they were a Christian sect. The Hindus in India could have made valuable allies against the real world-wide enemy, Islam, but the Portuguese never tried to come to terms with the Hindu mentality, or the Indian caste system, and relations worsened as the intolerant spirit of the Counter-Reformation spread throughout the empire. In 1540 a royal order was issued at Goa for the destruction of all Hindu temples. Subsequent regulations prevented any non-Christian from holding public office. After the arrival of St Francis Xavier and the first Jesuits at Goa in 1542 the proportion of ecclesiastics to laity within Portuguese establishments steadily expanded and the spirit of intolerance worsened (**28**). Such attitudes tended to increase Portuguese diplomatic isolation. For instance, in the mid-century the rich Hindu kingdom of Vijayanagar was attacked and dismembered by a league of central Indian Moslem states while the Portuguese looked on and did nothing; yet those same states then turned their attention to Goa, and in more than two years of fierce fighting (1569–71) came close to capturing it.

3 Spain I: Exploration

Columbus

Christopher Columbus's life and voyages are better documented than those of any other discoverer before the seventeenth century; this, however, has not prevented their being the subject of frequent and continuing historical controversy. The orthodox view is that he was a visionary cosmographer who believed that he could find a new route to Asia by sailing west, that he finally received the support of the Spanish sovereigns for this plan, and that in 1492 he set out for Cathay, but discovered America instead (**48**). However, several variations on this thesis have been put forward. For example, three quite recent ones are: that he was a Jewish convert who sailed in order to find a place of refuge for the persecuted Jews of Spain (**88**); that he was secretly a Portuguese agent in the pay of John II (**32**); that he knew all about America from Scandinavian sources, and was aiming to reach the Caribbean, not Asia (**71**).

Columbus was born in Genoa in 1451. His father, a weaver, was not particularly well-off, and Columbus's education was practical rather than academic, despite the later assertion of his son, Ferdinand, that he studied at the University of Padua. Columbus's lack of Italian in later life has caused some argument about his birthplace, but the explanation is that the Genoese dialect of the day was very different from standard Italian, which a poor boy growing up in Genoa would not have needed to acquire.

At an early age Columbus took to the sea. He made at least one voyage to the Levant as the employee of a Genoese bank. On another voyage his ship was sunk by a French privateer off Cape St Vincent and he swam ashore, eventually reaching Lisbon. For the next few years he may have worked in Portugal and Madeira as an agent of the same bank. He married a Portuguese lady of noble, though possibly illegitimate, birth named Felipa Perestrello. His wife's brother was governor of Porto Santo, a small island near Madeira, and Columbus may have lived on this island for some years. During this time he made at least one voyage to the Portuguese base of Elmina in Guinea, and he must have gained some knowledge of the latest Portuguese discoveries and techniques of navigation. Later he was to claim that he also visited Iceland, in 1477 (**90**). If this is true he may there have learnt something about the Atlantic, and lands to the west, from Scandinavian sources. Certainly there was trade, and even co-operation in exploration, between Portugal and Scandinavia during the fifteenth century. As far as Columbus is concerned, however, all this is conjectural unless and until new evidence comes to light.

In 1474 Columbus received an important letter from the Florentine cosmographer and scholar, Paolo Toscanelli [**doc. 20**]. It was the reply to an enquiry Columbus had made, and it consisted mainly of a copy of another, earlier, letter which Toscanelli had sent to a Portuguese correspondent, Fernão Martins, who was seeking information on behalf of King Alfonso V of Portugal. The letters explained that the best way to Asia was not round Africa but west across the Atlantic. Columbus clearly thought Toscanelli's views important, as he copied them out verbatim on to the flyleaf of one of his own cosmographical books. He later received a second letter in which Toscanelli noted his 'magnificent and grand desire to navigate from the parts of the east to the west', and wished him well.

These letters from an acknowledged authority must have given Columbus reassurance about the plan which was already germinating in his own mind. Toscanelli accepted Marco Polo's estimate of the extent of the landmass of Asia, and disagreed with Ptolemy's smaller estimate. He also computed a degree of latitude at the equator as equivalent to only 72 kilometres, which is 75 per cent of its actual length, and hence he underestimated the circumference of the earth. By using Toscanelli's calculations, and exaggerating them still further, Columbus reckoned that a mere 3,840 kilometres of ocean separated Cipangu (Japan) from the Canaries, the westernmost point of Europe. The actual distance is 16,960 kilometres. He must have brooded for years about the possibility of undertaking a voyage to Cipangu or Cathay. Two books from his personal collection which still survive are, significantly, the *Imago Mundi* of Cardinal d'Ailly, and the *Historia Rerum* of Aeneus Sylvius (Pope Pius II). Both these late medieval treatises support the idea of Asia being accessible from the west. 'It is evident', argued d'Ailly, 'that this sea [the Atlantic] is navigable in a very few days if the wind be fair' (**48**). From the numerous marginal comments in Columbus's own hand it is clear that he took these opinions very seriously. He became a man with a mission, convinced that God had destined him to undertake such a voyage. He also acquired an obsession about the wealth and honours which he, a foreigner from an obscure background, would deserve if he succeeded in reaching his goal. This is shown by the precise and detailed demands he made for himself to the various sovereigns whom he approached (**48, 73**).

In 1484 he put his scheme to John II of Portugal. John submitted it to his experts, who rejected it. They may have had adequate scientific grounds for so doing, but no doubt their main reason was that all Portugal's resources were involved at this point in the African route, which was starting to look promising after the return that year of Diego Cão from his first voyage. Columbus then went to Spain, but had returned to Lisbon by 1488, in time, possibly, to witness the return of Bartholemew Dias from the Cape of Good Hope. The circumnavigation of the Cape must have finally finished off any prospects Columbus had in Portugal, so he returned again to Spain, where he remained until successful.

The next six years were a period of difficulty for him. His wife had died, leaving him with a young son, Diego, to look after, and without the continuing support of the powerful Perestrello family. He importuned Ferdinand and Isabella with his plan, but he also dispatched his younger brother to England, and probably also to France, to plead his case. Bartholemew was a skilled cosmographer and map maker. He met Henry VII in 1489. Fernando Colón (Ferdinand Columbus) and Oviedo, biographers of Christopher Columbus, give brief but plausible accounts of what transpired, though they may have merely been filling in a historical gap. Oviedo says that Henry convened a committee to examine Bartholemew's proposals, and modern historians have speculated on who the members of such a committee might have been (**61**). In any case it seems the scheme was rejected. There is no record at all of what happened in France, or of what the regent, Anne of Beaujeu, thought. In Spain, however, after numerous refusals and long delays, Ferdinand and Isabella decided to give the scheme their backing. This was not because their advisers had suddenly become convinced of the correctness of Columbus's arguments, but because the royal treasurer, Luis de Santangel, decided to provide part of the financial backing necessary (**34**). Santangel was linked with a group of Genoese financiers operating through Seville, and he also controlled the finances of the powerful *Santa Hermandad*, a corporation responsible for civil order in Castile. The loan offered by him came from one or both of these sources – the evidence is not clear.

With a guaranteed loan Ferdinand had nothing to lose; he gave his royal backing for an expedition to be led by Columbus, and after that events moved rapidly. A legal contract between Columbus and the sovereigns, known as the *Capitulations*, was drawn up. This was later expanded into a longer document, the *Title* [**doc. 21**]. These conferred on Columbus the titles of Admiral of the Indies, and Viceroy. The former was not a naval rank but gave him administrative and judicial powers over the seas and lands which he might discover. He was also to be awarded the more honorific title of High Admiral of Castile, which was to be hereditary to his family. He was to receive a tenth of the value of all merchandise acquired in any way in the new lands. These clauses did not mention specific names of countries such as Cathay or Cipangu, a fact which has caused speculation that Columbus was not aiming to reach Asia at all, but to discover entirely new lands. However, the contract was a fairly typical one – similar in wording, for instance, to John Cabot's of 1496. Also Columbus received from the sovereigns *Letters of Credence*, to the rulers he would encounter, the terms of which show that they expected him to visit civilized communities, as Marco Polo had done: 'We have learnt with joy of your esteem and high regard for us and our nation, and of your great eagerness to be informed about things with us. Wherefore, we have resolved to send you our noble captain, Christopherus Colón, bearer of these' (**34**). Yet another indication that Columbus was expected to meet important princes was the inclusion in the expedition's membership of a converted Jew, Luis de Torres, who understood Hebrew and Arabic – the latter then believed to be the mother of all tongues. He was to interpret when Columbus encountered the Great Khan, or someone equally significant.

The *Capitulations* were signed in April 1492, two months after the fall of Granada, which may also account for Ferdinand and Isabella now having the time to attend to Columbus. In May he arrived at the small port of Palos in Andalusia, which was ordered, in punishment for certain misdemeanours, to provide two caravels for his use, for 12 months. Also, the province was told to furnish workmen and equipment at reasonable prices without local taxation. Palos produced the caravels *Niña* and *Pinta* at their taxpayers' expense, and Columbus himself charted the larger *Santa Maria* from its owner, Juan de la Cosa. We cannot be sure what these ships looked like. The caravels were each about 60 tonnes, tonnage referring to the cubic capacity of the hold in terms of wine tuns, or large casks. Morison has calculated that the two were each about 21 metres in overall length, 7 metres in beam, and not over 2 metres in draught (**48**). They were single-decked, but with a raised quarter-deck providing sleeping accommodation for the captain, and possibly the master. Their rig was probably three-masted and square-sailed, except that *Niña* started as lateen-rigged but was altered to square in the Canaries to take full advantage of the favourable prevailing wind. The *Santa Maria* may have been of about 100 tonnes, and was described in Columbus's *Journal* as a *não* (ship), not a caravel. She would have been more thick-set, less fast and graceful than the caravels. All three carried artillery – iron lombards, which were stone-throwing cannon of about 23 centimetres calibre, mounted on deck, as well as small falconets mounted on the bulwarks to repel boarders. Additionally, the crew had crossbows and primitive muskets. Living conditions were extremely primitive, with no proper cooking facilities, and no covered sleeping quarters, except perhaps for the officers.

It would be easy today to design more comfortable, labour-saving ships. However, Columbus's seamen probably fared as well as Spanish peasants on shore, except when rough weather prevented a fire for cooking. Also, for what they were, the three ships were well constructed; their builders had a long tradition of ocean-going experience behind them, experience of sail which has now been lost. It is interesting that when in 1892, to commemorate the voyage, Spain and the USA built replicas of the vessels and tried to have them sail across the Atlantic, the two caravels had to be towed, and even the *Santa Maria* had an extremely rough passage (**48**).

Exceptionally for a fifteenth-century expedition, almost the entire crew list and pay roll for the first voyage survives. The *Santa Maria* carried some 40 men, and the caravels about 25 each. There were no soldiers, and few gentlemen or hangers-on apart from the royal interpreter, de Torres. Most of the crew were professional seamen. The most important, after Columbus, were the members of the Pinzón family of Palos. Martin Alonzo Pinzón was a seaman of experience and local standing who was given command of *Pinta*, of which his younger brother became master, and another brother, Vincente Yanez Pinzón, commanded *Niña*. The fact that the family were prepared to back the voyage must have helped Columbus recruit sufficient men, something which was proving difficult. Immunity from legal actions was offered to all who volunteered, but only five took up the offer. It was after all a voyage into the totally unknown. Martin Alonzo Pinzón caused some trouble during the voyage, and died within days of arriving home, but this was not the end of the story. His family later brought a law suit against Columbus claiming that he, Martin, had been the real instigator and leader of the whole expedition, and Columbus a mere figurehead with court influence.

Columbus was captain of the *Santa Maria*; under him was the owner, Juan de la Cosa, as master. A man of the same name made a famous world map in 1500 and also led his own voyage of discovery to South America. There is some disagreement among historians as to whether this was in fact the same man, but the balance of opinion is that it was (**48, 86**). According to Columbus's *Journal* it was through de la Cosa's negligence that the *Santa Maria* was shipwrecked off Hispaniola [**doc. 23**].

The first voyage

Practically all that is known about this first voyage comes from the *Journal*, which is, in Morison's view, 'the most detailed, the most interesting and the most entrancing sea journal in history' (**48**). Unfortunately, the manuscript of the *Journal* has long since disappeared, and all that exists today is an abstract of it by the sixteenth-century historian, de las Casas, which, however, does contain long verbatim quotations from the original [**docs. 22, 23**] (**17**). There are also a few other quotations in the biography of Columbus by his son, Ferdinand.

Columbus set off from Palos on 3 August for the Canaries, from which, after a pause to re-stock and alter *Pinta's* rigging, he set sail on 6 September, steering due west. The reason why he went first to the Canaries is that these islands belonged to Spain, whereas the Azores, due west of Palos, were Portuguese. Also, he was aiming at Cathay, and in particular at the cities of Kinsai and Zaiton of which he had read in the pages of Marco Polo [**doc. 1**]. He probably possessed a map, perhaps one sent him by Toscanelli, which showed Zaiton as on the same latitude as the Canaries. Columbus was using the well-known navigational technique of sailing to the correct degree of latitude and then keeping to it by 'running down his westing' until he reached his destination. He was extremely lucky in that if he had attempted to cross the Atlantic from the Azores he would have been battling all the way against the prevailing Westerlies, and would probably have failed to make headway, as had no doubt many others, whereas from the Canaries he was just on the edge of the North-East Trade Wind zone. In fact, Columbus was inexperienced in the more sophisticated technique of celestial navigation. Occasionally during his voyages he tried to calculate his latitude with the quadrant, but almost invariably made errors, sometimes bad ones, as when he thought that the north coast of Cuba was 45 degrees north, when it is actually 21 degrees north. It was only during his fourth voyage, when he was marooned in Jamaica for nearly a year, that he attained any proficiency with the quadrant. However, it should be said that this technique was not yet regarded as part of the necessary qualifications for a professional seaman.

Ten days out from the Canaries patches of green seaweed were sighted. It was thought that land was close, but in fact they were on the edge of the immense Sargasso sea. From now on they were constantly anticipating signs of land, and making much of live crabs in the weed, floating branches, or birds of a kind which supposedly returned to roost on land at night. They made excellent speed before the north-easterly winds, but Columbus attempted to deceive his crew by each day reporting that the fleet had covered less distance than he really believed it had. Actually his calculations were inexact, and his faked distances were more accurate than his recorded ones. In spite of this precaution there came a point when the sailors started to complain about the length of the voyage, and to demand a return home. But Columbus's determination won the day. On 12 October, 33 days after leaving the Canaries, they sighted land in the shape of the tiny island of San Salvador in the Bahamas. The following morning Columbus went on shore with the royal standard and took formal possession of the island in the names of Ferdinand and Isabella. His *Journal* contains a detailed description of the natives, who were friendly and who afterwards surrounded the ship in their dug-out canoes [**doc. 22**]. These were the gentle and peaceable Caribs, very soon to be exterminated by Spanish settlers. From the first time he met them Columbus was thinking of the future – how easily these people could be converted to Christianity because they did not seem to have any religion of their own to speak of. He also notes how tractable and obedient they were; in other words how easy it would be make them into servants. This willingness of the natives, or Indians as they were called from now on, to fetch and carry for their new guests was a fatal characteristic. Before long every Spaniard must have been convinced that he need never do any physical work again, so long as he stayed in the New World.

By sign language the Spaniards soon made themselves understood. Some of the natives wore gold ornaments round their necks, and they rapidly came to realise that gold was an obsession with their new friends. There was a regional, though quite modest, source of gold in north-central Hispaniola, and by the end of the first voyage Columbus had come quite close to this area and succeeded in collecting a certain quantity of gold ornaments by barter. He had also convinced himself that he was on the threshold of the continent of Asia, and that huge gold deposits lay very near. Later, it was this frenzied search for gold which was to cause the ruin of the Caribs' fragile economy and social structure.

After threading their way past smaller islands the expedition arrived at Cuba, and sailed westwards along its northern coast for several days before returning on their tracks, and then crossing the windward passage to Hispaniola. On the evening of 24 December the *Santa Maria* ran aground on a reef and had to be abandoned [**doc. 23**]. A few days before this the *Pinta* under Martin Pinzón had sailed off on her own, against Columbus's orders, to search for gold. The shipwreck meant that there was no alternative but to set up a small fort using timber from the wreck, and leave behind 40 men while the rest crowded on to the *Niña* for the journey home. As they left Hispaniola they met *Pinta* again, and Columbus's *Journal* shows his anger at the behaviour of Pinzón, whom, however, he was in no position to discipline. On 16 January 1493 the two caravels set off, following, for the return voyage, a more northerly route which took advantage of the Westerlies. It was uneventful, except for a severe storm which again separated the two. Columbus put in at the Azores, where he had difficulties with the Portuguese authorities, but overcame them. On the final leg of the journey there was another storm which blew him off course so that he had to land in the estuary of the Tagus. He was allowed to proceed to Lisbon and there received a seemingly polite reception from King John, who must nevertheless have suspected that the voyage had infringed the Portuguese sphere of influence south of the Canaries. Perhaps Columbus produced his erroneous quadrant reading of 45 degrees north in order to reassure the king, but it is unlikely that the Portuguese cosmographers were taken in, During the interview John induced the Indians whom Columbus had brought back with him to demonstrate the positions of their islands with a handful of beans. In the event Columbus was allowed to proceed to Spain, but John immediately started up the diplomatic negotiations which were to lead to the Treaty of Tordesillas.

On 3 March, six months after his departure, Columbus returned to Palos. Martin Pinzón, who had also been blown off course, arrived on the same tide, but Ferdinand and Isabella would not allow him to present himself at court with his version of the events of the voyage, and he died shortly afterwards. Columbus on arrival sent off to the sovereigns a short acount which was later published, and is known as the *Letter* (**15, 18**). It confirms the general picture presented by the *Journal* – that he believed he had reached Asia, and that Cuba was part of the Asiatic mainland. He made much of the riches of the new lands, particularly the gold, and also, 'slaves, as many as they shall order'. It is clear that he never thought seriously about the peoples he had discovered except in terms of a master–slave relationship. This is not strange considering his experience of Portuguese West Africa and the Canaries, where slavery was the norm.

Ferdinand and Isabella were delighted with the results of the voyage, and honoured Columbus at court. The titles and privileges of the *Capitulations* were confirmed, and immediate proposals for another voyage approved, which, in view of the likely reaction from Portugal, was to leave without delay. At the same time negotiations with the Papacy started, to secure for Spain a monopoly of navigation and settlement in the lands Columbus had discovered. Alexander VI, already under an obligation to the Spanish monarchs, was co-operative. He issued a series of four Bulls following along the lines of their successive demands. The first two granted to Spain all lands discovered, or to be discovered, in areas explored by Columbus. The third, *Inter caetera*, drew a line of demarcation from north to south, 100 leagues (nearly 600 kilometres) west of the Cape Verde islands, and provided that everything west of this line was to belong to Spain. The fourth, *Dudum siquidem*, was vaguer but more sweeping. It cancelled previous rights given to other nations, which clearly included those given to Portugal by the Bulls of 1481 and 1455. These had granted to Portugal a sphere of influence south of an east–west line drawn through the Canaries. *Dudum siquidem* also extended previous grants to Spain by including 'all islands and mainlands whatever, found or to be found, . . . in sailing or travelling towards the west or south, whether they lie in regions occidental or meridional and oriental and of India' (**58**). The reference to India, and the principle of east–west demarcation presented a serious threat to Portugal. If Columbus were now to reach Asia by sailing westwards, before the Portuguese reached it by sailing eastwards, *Dudum siquidem's* terms meant that Portugal would lose all the fruits of her painfully pursued explorations. John II therefore used all his resources to challenge the papal rulings, including the spreading of rumours that he was about to send a great fleet under Almeida to assert his rights in the Atlantic. The upshot was direct negotiations between Spain and Portugal which resulted in the Treaty of Tordesillas of 1494, whereby the line of *Inter caetera* was moved a further 270 leagues to the west [**doc. 24**]. This meant that Spain agreed to leave to Portugal the entire eastern route to India, as well as the coast of Brazil, although the existence of the latter was probably not yet known.

Later voyages

Before the treaty was signed Columbus was back in the West Indies. He left in September 1493, with a fleet of 17 ships. There were 1,500 people on board, *hidalgos* (gentlemen), artisans, soldiers, clerks, farmers, together with equipment for building and for farming. It was a microcosm of male Spanish society, and the intention was to colonise Hispaniola – although there were no women in the expedition – making a self-sufficient base from which further exploration could be conducted. The fleet made a good passage, but on arrival they found that the earlier settlement of Navidad with its 40 men had been wiped out. Columbus founded a new city, Isabela, though the site he chose was unsuitable and later had to be changed. The new settlement proved extremely difficult to govern, especially as Columbus was more interested in the search for Cathay and soon left to explore the south coast of Cuba and to discover Jamaica. On his return, without much to show, he met with disaffection and a state of open war between the settlers and the natives, who were exasperated at the demands made on them for gold, food and women. The Spaniards had imposed a regular gold levy which the Indians were quite unable to meet. Before Columbus's arrival gold had played little part in their economy, and the small nuggets used for ornaments had been collected over generations. These were quickly made over to the Spaniards, who pressed for more. But there was little more forthcoming; the Indians had neither the techniques nor the habits of labour needed for working major deposits. The Spanish answer to the lack of gold was brutality and enslavement; thousands of Indians were killed and hundreds shipped to Spain, where they died quickly.

In 1496 Columbus left Isabela in charge of his brother, Bartholemew, and sailed to Spain to answer the complaints that malcontents were bringing back from Hispaniola. In his absence Bartholemew organised the evacuation of the site and the building of a new city, Santo Domingo, which survives to this day. Columbus now desperately needed a successful voyage which would either prove conclusively that Asia had been reached, or would tap a really rich source of gold. The Spanish sovereigns were becoming increasingly, and rightly, doubtful about his capacities as a colonial administrator, but they allowed him another chance to explore. This time he sailed well to the south of his former discoveries, and arrived at Trinidad. He explored, but did not personally set foot on, the northern shore of the Gulf of Parias, on the South American mainland. A great volume of fresh water entering the sea, actually one of the mouths of the Orinoco, was thought by Columbus to be possibly one of the four great rivers of the Earthly Paradise described in Genesis. Unfortunately he just missed discovering the pearl fishery of Margarita, north-west of Trinidad. From Parias he crossed the Caribbean and arrived at Santo Domingo, to find that some of the settlers had rebelled against Bartholemew. In order to placate the settlers, and compensate them for the lack of gold, Columbus started to make grants of land, or *repartimientos*, to individual Spaniards. These soon came to mean the right of ownership not only of a specific area but also of all the Indians living within it. The Indians were thereby placed at the entire disposal of their new master, who could exploit them in any way he wished. This was the birth of the *encomienda* system which later spread to Mexico and Peru and became for half a century the semi-feudal basis of Spanish rule in the New World.

The new grants did not improve the mood of the settlers, or their relationship with the Columbus brothers, who were resented as foreign upstarts. There were complaints by homeward-bound officials of their vacillating and tyrannical administration, and Isabella was also increasingly disturbed by the reports she received of the inhuman treatment of the Indians. Columbus by now was deteriorating both mentally and physically. He suffered delusions of persecution and grandeur, believing that his enemies were also those of God (**48**). Finally, in 1499, the sovereigns appointed Francisco de Bobadilla to supersede Columbus and investigate complaints against him. Bobadilla acted ruthlessly and hastily, sending the brothers back to Spain in chains, and after this Columbus was never again allowed to set foot in Hispaniola, although Isabella released him from custody on his arrival in Spain and he retained his property rights.

By this time it had become clear that Portugal had won the race to Asia. Vasco da Gama returned from Calicut in 1499, and in 1500

Cabral was dispatched with a large fleet to India, which he reached after landing on the coast of Brazil *en route*. Ferdinand and Isabella's decision to allow Columbus yet one more chance to discover a western route to Asia was a somewhat desperate last effort to counter Portugal's success and reach the source of the spices first. Columbus set off on his fourth voyage in 1502, to look for a way through the island archipelago which he had discovered, to the Asian mainland that he still believed lay nearby. He hoped to find a passage south of Cuba and Hispaniola, but north of Trinidad and the Earthly Paradise of his third voyage.

Columbus's fourth voyage was his longest, lasting 30 months, and it was a voyage of heroism, peril and missed opportunities. He traversed practically the entire Atlantic coastline of Central America, from Cape Honduras in the north to the Gulf of Darien in the south. He narrowly missed making contact with the rich Mayan culture of Yucatan, failing to follow up a chance encounter with a long canoe loaded with Mayan merchandise. And because by now he was rigidly and inflexibly pursuing one idea only, that of finding a sea passage to Asia, he failed to make contact with Indians who could have told him of the existence of the Pacific Ocean only a few miles away across the isthmus of Panama. As it was, unexpected storms, fierce fights with Indian tribes and mutiny made the voyage a total disaster. After having to abandon their only remaining vessel, rotten with sea-worm, the surviving Spaniards were marooned for nearly a year on the coast of Jamaica, an island as yet unsettled by Europeans. By this time Columbus had become mentally quite unfit for command, and they were only saved through the resolution of Bartholemew, who became the *de facto* leader. Back in Spain Columbus's reception was less than lukewarm, and the death of his patroness, Isabella, in 1504, was the final blow. He himself died two years later, worn out and querulous, though still rich from his continuing share of Indies trade. His reputation and honour were maintained by his two sons, the scholar Ferdinand, who wrote his biography, and Diego, who became an effective governor of Hispaniola.

Columbus's character was complex. His megalomanic insistence that he alone understood the mysteries of cosmology, his total refusal to compromise, and his insistence on an almost monarchical personal status (**73**), were traits which became more pronounced as his luck ran out towards the end of his career. He has been described as 'a self-educated, emotional, unpopular man, prone to self-pity, who clung tenaciously to a quite mistaken cosmographical theory'

(**15**). Nevertheless, he was a figure of heroic proportions, who had the vision to grasp a great idea, and the single-minded determination to see it through. His mind was a mixture of medieval and modern: medieval in that he arrived at his theory by a mixture of deductive reasoning and faith; modern in his ability to translate thought into action, his thirst for adventure, and his curiosity. About his capacity as a navigator there has been much argument. His best-known biographer, Morison, sees him as the greatest dead-reckoning navigator of the age (**48**); others have described him as an undistinguished navigator who acquired what experience and knowledge he did have from Portuguese experts (**15**). In support of the former view there is his feat during the third voyage of steering a course from Trinidad to Hispaniola across totally unknown waters. But it must be conceded that he knew little about navigation by the stars.

Vespucci

By the time Columbus had been sent back to Spain by Bobadilla, the monopoly of exploration granted to him in the *Capitulations* of 1492 had been broken. In 1499 two ex-companions of his, Alonso de Hojeda and Juan de la Cosa, together with an Italian, Amerigo Vespucci, left Cadiz for Trinidad, from where they explored the coast of Venezuela, discovering the pearl fishery missed by Columbus. After a period in Hispaniola they returned home with a cargo of slaves snatched from the Bahamas. Following this voyage la Cosa may have drafted his famous world map, which is the earliest surviving map to show the New World (**51, 86**). The la Cosa map provides some sort of yardstick as to how much of the American coastline was known by 1500. It shows a continuous continental coastline from what may be the lands discovered by John Cabot in the north to Brazil in the south. The only gap is in the Panama region, where the coast is interrupted by a strategically placed picture of St Christopher, leaving open the question of the existence of a through passage to Asia. The dating and draughtmanship of the map are unsettled; one recent theory is that Vespucci had a hand in it (**72**).

Vespucci was a Florentine businessman who took to the sea comparatively late in life. He probably made two voyages, the one mentioned and another, of 1501, under Portuguese auspices, in which he followed up Cabral's discovery of Brazil by exploring the coast of South America southwards, perhaps as far as Patagonia.

He must have made himself into a reasonably competent geographer and navigator, as during the last seven years of his life (1505–12) he held the office of Chief Pilot to the *Casa de Contratación* at Seville [**doc. 25**]. However, to set against this there is the verdict of the Brazilian historian, Duarte Leite: 'In truth Vespucci was a cunning Florentine, vain, ambitious and with a superficial knowledge of exact sciences' (**51**). His voyages received great publicity during his lifetime, and two pamphlets, the *Mundus Novus*, and the *Quattuor Navigationes* in particular, both bearing his name but probably not written by him, received very wide circulation. The latter ascribes to him voyages which he almost certainly did not undertake, but its importance lies in the fact that a German, Martin Waldseemüller, wrote an introduction to its 1507 edition in which he suggested that Vespucci's name should be given to the new lands. Vespucci himself was undoubtedly an astute and articulate publicist, and thus he gained the fame which was really due to Columbus (**51, 57**).

One question about Vespucci is whether he did in fact realise that the coastline which he explored belonged to a new continent. Key passages in his letters suggest that he did [**doc. 26**], but this is debatable, partly because he may not have written them, partly because the terms 'continent' and 'new world' did not necessarily carry their modern connotations (**87**). He may have thought that South America was part of the long peninsula which contemporary maps based on Ptolemy showed as stretching south from Cathay, separating the Atlantic from the Indian Ocean. Vespucci's use of Ptolemaic nomenclature seems to bear this out. In fact the belief that the new lands were in some way connected to Asia took a long time to die out. Waldseemüller himself, who had credited Vespucci with the discovery of a new continent, later changed his mind and made at least a partial retreat to Ptolemaic cosmology. And even Magellan, who rounded South America in 1519, probably believed that he was rounding the aforesaid Ptolemaic peninsula, rather than a separate new continent. It was only when the survivors of Magellan's expedition returned to Spain, having circumnavigated the globe, that the old theory became untenable, and even after that cartographers continued in many cases to show Asia and America joined up by a huge bridge of land in the north (**87**).

The decade prior to Magellan's voyage of 1519 was one of increasing rivalry between Spain and Portugal over the Atlantic coastline of South America. Brazil had been discovered for Portugal by Cabral in April 1500, on his way to India, and had been named by him 'Land of the True Cross'. However, Vincente Yanez Pinzón, the Andalusian captain of *Niña* on Columbus's first voyage, had also led a voyage to Brazil from Palos the same year. It is likely that Pinzón made landfall near the modern city of Recife, in January 1500, before sailing north-west for the Gulf of Parias and, finally, Santo Domingo, which he reached in June (**51**). Thus Spain had at least an equal claim to have reached this coast first. Spain admitted that the Tordesillas line of demarcation gave Cabral's landfall to Portugal, but argued that Cabral had merely discovered an island, and that the entire coastline of the mainland behind belonged to Spain. Portugal, on the other hand, claimed the coast from Cape St Roque at about latitude 5 degrees south, where Cabral had landed, to latitude 50 degrees south, the point that Vespucci claimed to have reached on the 1501 voyage. By this time, too, this coast was becoming commercially important for the logwood, or brazilwood, which, when processed, produced red and black washable dyes. This commodity was to give its name to the new country, and was another cause of Iberian rivalry. By 1519 Portugal had established two factories where the trees were felled and cut up ready for shipment home each summer.

In 1508 Ferdinand sent an expedition commanded jointly by Pinzón and Juan de Solis to search for the strait which was still believed to separate the newly discovered continental coastline from the Ptolemaic peninsula to the south. Solis was given a spell in prison when he returned empty-handed from this voyage, but by 1512 he had clearly regained favour as in that year he became Chief Pilot, following the death of Vespucci. In 1515 he received another command, and on this occasion sailed down as far as the estuary of the River Plate, which he explored and which for some years was named after him. Unfortunately, on seeing some apparently friendly natives on the shore he incautiously landed with seven men, whereupon: 'sodenly a great multitude of the inhabitants bruist forth upon them, and slue them every man with clubbes, even in the sight of their fellows, not one escaping. Their furie not thus satisfied, they cut the slayne men in peeces, even upon the shore, where their fellows might behold this horrible spectacle from the sea. . .' (**51**).

Magellan

Fernão de Magalhães, or Ferdinand Magellan as his name is anglicised, was, with Columbus and da Gama, one of the three greatest explorers of the age, and of the three he has some claim to be called the greatest. He overcame mutiny and starvation to cross the Pacific

Ocean, until then totally unknown, and was responsible for, though he did not himself live to complete, the first circumnavigation of the earth (**22, 51**).

He was of the Portuguese lesser nobility, the class which furnished the leadership for the earlier voyages, and as a young man he saw service with the first Portuguese viceroy to India, Francisco de Almeida, accompanying him out east in 1505. Little is known of Magellan's early career in India, but the fact that he travelled as far east as Banda in the Moluccas justifies the claim that he was the first human being to circle the globe, because Banda is at longitude 130 degrees east, whereas the Philippines, where he was killed, are at 124 degrees east.

After his return from India, Magellan became interested in the idea of finding a faster route to the Spice Islands than round the Cape of Good Hope. He was certain that they could be reached by following Columbus's original plan of sailing westwards. However, King Manuel, to whom the plan was submitted, was unimpressed. It seems that about the same time Magellan asked for, and was refused, an increase in salary. Furthermore he was also in trouble over a charge arising from military service. He had volunteered to serve with Portuguese forces in Morocco but had subsequently been accused of selling surrendered cattle back to the enemy. These events must have been factors in his decision to leave Portugal and seek service under the Spanish crown, which he did in 1517, at the age of 37. He submitted his scheme for a western voyage to the *Casa de Contratación* [**doc. 34**]. By now he had also worked out that if the line of Tordesillas were extended to the other side of the globe it would leave the Spice Islands on the eastern, or Spanish, side. This was in fact not true. A line 370 leagues (each nearly 6 kilometres) west of the Cape Verde Islands would be at longitude 45 degrees 30 minutes west. Extended to the other side of the globe the line becomes 130 degrees 30 minutes east, which leaves the Spice Islands, the Philippines and almost all of Indonesia on the Portuguese side. However, it should be emphasized that neither Magellan nor anyone else at that time had any means of measuring longitude, so his theory could hardly be substantiated one way or another. Nor was there any way of knowing the width of the ocean between the Pacific coastline, first discovered by Balboa in 1513 [**doc. 31**], and the Spice Islands. In any event, Charles I of Spain (soon to become, in addition, emperor, as Charles V) was presumably impressed with Magellan's reasoning since he signed a charter giving him possession of all new lands that he might discover within the Spanish domain save for the Spice Islands themselves, five of which were to belong to the crown, and the next two to Magellan.

In September 1519, Magellan set sail in command of five ships. One of them, the *San Antonio*, was commanded by Juan de Cartagena, who turned out to be a thorn in Magellan's flesh. He owed his appointment to the fact that he was the 'nephew', i.e. the bastard, of Bishop Fonseca, the most influential member of the *Casa de Contratación*. One important foreigner on Magellan's flagship, the *Trinidad*, was Antonio Pigafetta, from Vicenza, who wrote a detailed, though highly coloured, journal of the expedition [**docs. 35, 36**] (**22**). There were few Portuguese in the fleet; like Columbus, Magellan was surrounded by foreigners. They avoided the direct course to Brazil in order to give the slip to any intercepting Portuguese squadrons, and instead sailed down the coast of Africa before crossing the Atlantic and running into equatorial calms. During this difficult time Magellan suppressed a short mutiny led by Cartagena, and had him demoted from his command.

The fleet spent two weeks resting and re-provisioning at Rio de Janeiro (which had been given this name, i.e. 'River of January', by Vespucci, who first entered the bay in January 1502). They then leisurely reconnoitred the coast of Patagonia, taking nearly five weeks to reach Port St Julian, at 49 degrees south. Here, Magellan was faced by his second, and more serious, mutiny, involving three of the five ships. This was crushed by a mixture of cunning and audacity; several ringleaders were either hanged or, like Cartagena, marooned – which was no less certain a way to die. Shortly afterwards one of the ships grounded and had to be abandoned, but in October 1520 the remainder discovered and entered the Strait of Magellan between the Patagonian mainland and the island of Tierra del Fuego, or 'Land of Fire', so named by Magellan because of the nightly signal fires lit by natives whom they never encountered. According to Pigafetta, Magellan 'knew where to sail to find a well-hidden strait, which he saw depicted on a map in the treasury of the king of Portugal, made by that excellent man, Martin de Bohemia'. Biographers of Magellan have discussed the question of what map this was. It may have been one that showed a strait between South America and the supposed Antarctic continent running around the world, and perhaps joined up with China, in Ptolemaic style. The two features which such a map is unlikely to have shown, and which Magellan himself had painfully to discover, were the strait's extreme southerly position, and the vast width of the ocean between it and the Spice Islands.

The passage through the strait was a nightmare, and took 38 days. Even today the 474 kilometre waterway is one of the remotest, least inhabited and most dangerous in the world, although used regularly not only by ships going to Chile and Peru but by mammoth oil tankers too large for the Panama Canal. One of Magellan's ships, the *San Antonio*, disobeyed him and returned to Spain, but by the end of November 1520 the remaining three had emerged into the Pacific. Magellan steered a course northwards, keeping within 80 kilometres of the Chilean coast, until at 32 degrees south he set a course west-north-west. This was surprising, as he must have been aware that it would eventually take him far north of the Spice Islands. A recent interpretation of his motives suggests that he was intending to go precisely where he eventually arrived, namely the Philippines (**75**). The argument is that he had learnt when he was previously stationed in the east, possibly from Chinese traders, something unknown to any other Europeans. This was the secret of how to navigate a ship from the Spice Islands back to Spanish America. The wind system of the Pacific made this feat extremely difficult, and in fact it was not achieved by a Spaniard until Urdaneta in 1565. The only way to do it was to sail from the Spice Islands northwards to the Philippines, and then, using the South-West Monsoon, sail further north until about 40 degrees north, before picking up the Westerlies for California. Magellan, it is thought, wanted to establish cordial relations with native chiefs in the Philippines in order to secure a return passage. He may in fact have planned to set up a regular trading route between Mexico and the Spice Islands, aiming to bring spices to Spain so as to rival the established Portuguese route round Africa.

Whether this interpretation of his motives is correct or not, it is true that Magellan sailed considerably to the north of the Spice Islands, arriving, after terrible privations, at Guam in the Marianas. According to Pigafetta they were three months and 20 days without taking on fresh food or water. Scurvy was rife, and 19 men died of it in the three ships: 'We ate biscuit which was no longer biscuit but its powder, swarming with worms, the rats having eaten all the good. It stank strongly of their urine. We drank yellow water already many days putrid. We also ate certain ox hides that had covered the top of the yards to prevent the yards from chafing the shrouds, and which had become exceedingly hard because of the sun, rain and wind. We soaked them in the sea for four or five days, then placed them for a short time over the hot embers and ate them, and often we ate sawdust. Rats were sold for half a ducat apiece . . .'

(**22**). Magellan named the islands they eventually arrived at the Ladrones, meaning Thief Islands, because swarms of natives descended on them and stole every item not nailed down, even including one ship's longboat.

A week after leaving the Ladrones, or Marianas, as they were later renamed, they reached the Philippines. At Cebu they spent a delightful week being entertained by the chief, who became Magellan's blood brother and also received Christian baptism together with several hundred followers. However, Magellan rashly insisted on cementing the friendship by helping his new ally defeat an enemy on the neighbouring island of Mactan. He personally led three boatloads of Spaniards in a beachhead landing against a waiting native force. 'We begged him repeatedly not to go', wrote Pigafetta, 'but he, like a good shepherd, refused to abandon his flock'. In the ensuing fight Magellan made every possible mistake. He chose an unsuitable beach where the boats could not get within shooting distance of the shore, made no attempt at surprise, and failed to co-ordinate his attack with his native allies. The result was that his force of 48 was surrounded by about 1,500 natives, and Magellan himself, refusing to retreat, was hacked to death [**doc. 36**].

Further disasters awaited the remaining members of the expedition. Twenty-seven were killed by their native hosts after having been invited to a feast. One of the three ships had to be abandoned since there were now insufficient men to crew it. The *Trinidad* attempted to sail east but had to turn back in the face of contrary winds, finally surrendering to the Portuguese. The third ship, the *Victoria*, commanded by El Cano, left the Moluccas with 65 men and, after a long and harrowing voyage across the Indian Ocean, reached Seville with 19 men left, on 6 September 1522, three years and one month from their day of departure.

They were received graciously by Charles V, particularly as the 25 tonnes of cloves and the packets of cinnamon, mace and nutmeg brought back in the *Victoria's* hold more than paid for the entire cost of the expedition. El Cano received a pension and an appropriate coat of arms. The blazon included two crossed cinnamon sticks, three nutmegs and twelve cloves supported on each side by Malay kings each holding a branch of a spice tree. The motto was '*Primus circumdedisti me*' (You have first encompassed me).

Apart from being a stupendous feat of both navigation and endurance, Magellan's voyage was important geographically as it gave practical demonstration of the fact that the world was round, and also exploded the prevailing belief that the area of land on the globe far exceeded that of water. The vast width of the Pacific was now appreciated for the first time. However, if Magellan did know the secret of how to return across the Pacific from the Spice Islands, and if this secret died with him, then surely he was guilty of criminal negligence in not imparting it to others before he died. As El Cano said later, in Spain, Magellan 'had abandoned the armada to its fate' (**51**).

Charles V authorised two subsequent expeditions in an attempt to follow up Magellan's achievement and to further what may have been his original plan to establish a permanent trade link between the Spice Islands and America. In 1525 El Cano set off again, this time as pilot under Francisco de Loaysa, with a brief to establish a trading factory in the Moluccas. They went through the Strait of Magellan and crossed the Pacific to Guam. There a war started between the Spanish and Portuguese, each allied to certain native chiefs. Also, in 1527, Cortés, who had completed his conquest of Mexico, built three ships on the Pacific coast of Mexico and dispatched them under a kinsman of his, Saavedra. Two of the three were lost, but the third collected a cargo of cloves. However, as usual, it failed to make the return journey to Mexico, owing to contrary winds.

In any case, by this time Charles V had changed his policy regarding the Spice Islands. Faced by pressures from Suleiman the Magnificent on the Danube, and also by the French-inspired League of Cognac in Italy, he decided to cut his losses. He made the Treaty of Saragossa with Portugal in 1529, whereby he renounced his claims to the Spice Islands in return for 350,000 gold ducats. It was a wise move because the Portuguese were too strong in that area to be defeated, and hence Charles gained something for nothing. Moreover, the Philippines were left out of the treaty. In 1542 another Spanish expedition from Mexico, led by Villalobos, crossed the Pacific and formally claimed the Philippines, naming them after Charles's son Philip, later Philip II. In 1565 a Spanish ship finally discovered Magellan's alleged secret, how to sail from the Philippines to Mexico. The sequel to these achievements was an annual trade between Manila and Acapulco, thus eventually realising the original dream of Columbus.

4 SPAIN II: Conquest

Cortés

In 1509 Diego Columbus, son of Christopher, arrived in Santo Domingo as governor of the Indies. Two years later he sent Diego Velasquez with 300 men to conquer Cuba, still virtually unexplored. Between then and 1519, the date Cortés arrived in Mexico, knowledge about the Gulf of Mexico was gradually built up by a series of Spanish expeditions.

During 1517–18 there were two voyages to Yucatan which returned with gold, and stories about a large inland empire with stone-built cities, vast wealth, and a god-like ruler. The stage was now set for Cortés's epic expedition. Hernando Cortés had been only 26 when, as a treasurer's clerk, he had accompanied Velasquez in his conquest of Cuba. He was granted a *repartimiento* of Indians by Velasquez but, being a highly ambitious young man, realised that real power and wealth could only be achieved by an independent command and the successful conquest of further lands. In 1519 Cortés, now connected to Velasquez by marriage, was appointed by him to lead a third expedition to Yucatan. The governor subsequently became alarmed and jealous at the scope and thoroughness of Cortés's preparations, so he had to leave Cuba in a hurry before his instructions were countermanded. He sailed first to Trinidad, now entirely settled by the Spanish, to recruit more men, and then, in February 1519, set off for Mexico with 11 ships, some 600 Spaniards and 16 horses.

There is a considerable amount of information available to historians about Cortés's achievement, much more there is for Pizarro's conquest of Peru. The three main chronicles are by Gomara, Las Casas and Bernal Diaz del Castillo. The first two are rather biased – Gomara, who was Cortés's personal secretary, being highly favourable, while Las Casas, who took up the cause of the native 'Indians', was highly critical. However, Bernal Diaz's very long narrative, although written many years after the events, is factual and honest. He served throughout with Cortés and his memory for detail at the age of 70 remained excellent (**11, 45**).

Cortés was a complex character, who combined qualities rarely seen together – the forceful personality and personal courage of a leader with the cunning and forethought of a trained lawyer and strategist (**77**). From the beginning his behaviour was different from that of other leaders of expeditions. He tried, successfully, to weld his men into a disciplined force. Both a pilot who took one of the ships off course, and a group of soldiers who looted an Indian village, were severely punished.

After leaving Trinidad the expedition rounded the Yucatan peninsula and landed at Tabasco, where an initial skirmish with natives took place before water and food could be had. One result of this was a placatory gift to Cortés by the local *cacique*, or chief, of 20 women, whom Cortés distributed to his captains – after they had been baptised. One of the women was a chief's daughter, beautiful and intelligent, who was given the name Marina. She spoke Nahuatal, which turned out to be the language of the Aztecs, and, as she quickly learnt Spanish, she became the expedition's interpreter. According to Diaz her courage and presence of mind several times were to save Cortés's life.

The expedition finally landed on a small island off the Mexican coast, where later the port of St John of Ulua was built. There Cortés first heard about the great emperor of the Aztecs, Montezuma, and about Tenochtitlan, his fabulous capital city far in the interior. Nearby, the Spaniards founded a settlement, Vera Cruz, which was constituted as a legal city with its own government. Cortés's knowledge of the law came in useful here because a Spanish New World city owed allegiance only to the crown; Cortés was anticipating attempts by Velasquez in Cuba to recall or take over the expedition.

A few miles inland, in the native town of Zempoala, the Spaniards first encountered Aztec tax collectors. Cortés's ruthless treatment of these haughty representatives of Montezuma, whom he imprisoned, gained him the respect of the local Totonac Indians, who resented their subservience to the Aztecs. Another of Cortés's actions at this time is rightly famous as an impressive piece of conquistador theatre. He had all the ships they had come in sunk, thus ensuring that no one had any alternative but to follow him into the interior of Mexico.

In August 1519 Cortés set out for Tenochtitlan, leaving a garrison at Vera Cruz. Few can ever have embarked on a more hazardous venture. There were less than 400 of them and their goal lay some 400 kilometres away, across totally unknown and probably hostile territory, which turned out to include three great mountain ranges. This Aztec empire which he was now to cross was not really a unified kingdom but a loose federation of tribes dominated by the Aztecs who exacted tribute from, but did not directly govern, various subject tribes such as Totonacs, Toltecs and Mixtecs. Over the previous centuries these peoples had made their cultural contributions to a civilization that was in some ways as advanced as Renaissance Europe, although its technology was deficient in vital respects. They had no written language – messages were conveyed in a system of picture writing. Their masonry was accomplished, and their temples rivalled the Egyptian pyramids, but they had not developed the wheel nor the smelting of iron, though highly skilled at working gold and silver. Aztec swords and daggers had blades of obsidian. There were no beasts of burden and the horse was totally unknown.

Most startling to the Spaniards when they encountered it was the Aztec religion, a mixture of cruelty and superstition far exceeding the excesses of the Spanish Inquisition. On holy days thousands of captives – usually, but not always, prisoners-of-war – stood in queues waiting to mount the steps of temples so that priests could cut open their chests and rip out their hearts, to be offered up to the Aztec gods. One factor operating to the advantage of the Spanish was the desire of every Aztec warrior in battle to capture as many prisoners as possible for sacrifice, rather than kill the enemy. More than once Cortés was saved by his men while being dragged away from the battlefield by Aztecs who could have finished him off.

Like the Incas, Aztecs gave absolute obedience to their emperor. Montezuma's authority was so unquestioned that he continued to be obeyed long after he had become the prisoner and pawn of the Spaniards. The enigma of Cortés's fantastic success is related to Montezuma's character. He seems to have been both likeable and intelligent, but rapidly became dominated by Cortés's stronger, more ruthless, personality. It is also likely that Montezuma believed, or half believed, that Cortés was the re-incarnation of one of the Aztec gods. Quetzlcoatl, the plumed serpent god, was said to have left Mexico generations before, promising that he would one day return. Cortés's arrival coincided with the year in the Aztec calendar sacred to this god. Such a myth might account for Montezuma's hesitant and contradictory treatment of his unwelcome visitors. As they approached Tenochtitlan he repeatedly sent them rich presents and begged them to return home. He then tried, unsuccessfully, to have them ambushed. Finally he fatalistically invited them in to the city, showering them with honours and hospitality.

The most dangerous part of Cortés's march to Tenochtitlan was his attempt to cross the territory of the Tlaxcalans. This warlike tribe had never taken kindly to Aztec rule and had a long history of resistance. They fought against the Spanish to the limit of their powers, and only after a series of battles did Cortés succeed in reaching the city of Tlaxcala [**doc. 27**]. However, they then sued for peace, deciding that an alliance with the newcomers was their only hope of breaking the hated Aztec power. From this moment they became staunch allies, never wavering in their allegiance. If Cortés had not been able to fall back on Tlaxcala after the subsequent disastrous retreat from Tenochtitlan he would certainly have been overwhelmed by the Aztecs; as it was he was given a breathing space in which to plan his final assault on the capital.

Cortés finally arrived at Tenochtitlan, a breathtakingly beautiful city of some 60,000 houses, set on an island in the middle of Lake Texcoco, and accessible only by long causeways across the water. He was welcomed by Montezuma and his nobles and ushered to a palace next to the emperor's own. This became the Spaniards' home for the next few months [**doc. 28, 29**].

The following weeks were difficult for Cortés. He had achieved his goal and was in the capital, being treated almost as a conqueror. Yet it was a victory without substance. They were there as guests of Montezuma, and if his benevolence should evaporate, the city, surrounded as it was entirely by water, could become a trap. The news that Vera Cruz was under attack by Aztec warriors provided a pretext allowing Cortés to act. With about 30 followers he burst into the royal apartments, accused Montezuma of double-crossing him, and insisted that he should return with them to the Spanish quarters. From now on Montezuma was a closely guarded prisoner, allowed to perform his public duties only under escort. The Spaniards had ceased to be guests and were now puppet-masters, manipulating the emperor as they wanted. The Aztec noble responsible for the attack on the Spanish settlement was brought to Tenochtitlan and burnt alive outside the palace. Large quantities of gold and silver ornaments were handed over to the Spaniards, to be barbarously melted down into ingots so that Cortés and Charles V could each receive their fifth share. Cortés became so confident during these weeks that he even launched an assault on the Aztec religion, destroying images and washing away the caked blood of decades of human sacrifice from temple steps.

This honeymoon period ended when news came that Spanish ships had been seen near Vera Cruz. Cortés knew that these were not reinforcements but enemies, sent by Velasquez to supplant him. Leaving Pedro de Alvarado in charge of Montezuma he took most of his army back to the coast and launched an immediate attack. Although the newcomers were in the majority, Cortés's seasoned campaigners achieved a complete, though by careful calculation a fairly bloodless, victory, and the upshot was that Cortés gained many valuable recruits. But there was no time to celebrate because he now learnt that the hotheaded Alvarado had precipitated a revolt in Tenochtitlan by firing on a crowd of Indians noisily celebrating a religious festival. The situation was desperate. Cortés rushed back the 400 kilometres from the coast, to join Alvarado, under siege in his palace from a host of Indians. By now a new Aztec emperor had emerged to replace Montezuma, who in any case met his death during this siege. After some days it became clear that the capital would have to be abandoned. There followed what the Spanish chroniclers call the *Noche Triste*, when a night retreat turned into a rout, and over 600 Spaniards were killed, many because they were too loaded up with gold loot to defend themselves effectively. Even so, there were enough Spaniards, and especially enough horses, left to defeat the Aztecs when they made the mistake of launching an attack on an open plain where cavalry could be deployed to enormous effect. The battle of Otumba, of July 1520, was a victory which allowed the Spanish to fall back on the friendly city of Tlaxcala, there to bind their wounds and recover their spirits. By the end of the year Cortés was ready to march again. He had also built 13 small ships to operate on the lake of Texcoco and assist the advance up the causeways.

All was now set for the final act. This involved a vast and protracted assault on Tenochtitlan by the Spaniards, assisted by upwards of 100,000 native allies from tribes such as the Tlaxcalans who saw them as liberators. During 93 days of continuous fighting they first captured the villages round the lake, thus cutting off the Aztecs' food and fresh water supplies. Then the causeways were gained in bitter hand-to-hand combat. Finally the city was reduced and the houses destroyed, street by street. The Aztecs fought desperately against an enemy whose weapons they could never match. Towards the end thousands of emaciated bodies littered the city and the stench of rotting flesh was everywhere. Cortés had gained a ghost town which had to be entirely rebuilt, under its new name of Mexico City [**doc. 30**].

Cortés was now absolute ruler of a vast slice of Central America, an area much larger than Spain itself. Over the next few years the Pacific regions of modern Mexico were conquered, and also the Bay of Honduras and the Mayan cities of Guatemala. In these areas Spaniards exploring southwards encountered others moving northwards, sent by the governor of Darien. In 1522 Cortés's position was made official when Charles V appointed him governor of New Spain (Mexico). In three years a great civilization had disappeared, leaving few traces and Spain had gained an empire. Cortés's plans for New Spain were deeply influenced by his experiences in the Caribbean where he had seen the Indian population destroyed. He did not want this experience repeated in Mexico, and he wrote of the conservation of the Indians as being 'the cement on which all the work has to be built' (**77**). He had a vision of a vast empire, based on humanistic values, and stretching across the Pacific to Cathay. This vision was strongly influenced by Franciscan missionaries who appeared in Mexico shortly after the conquest. However, all such ambitions came to nought as the new governor became increasingly frustrated by royal officials dispatched from Madrid.

Pizarro

Before Cortés landed on the Mexican coast, other Spaniards had penetrated across the narrow isthmus of Darien. In 1513, Balboa reached the Pacific, wading into the water with drawn sword to claim the unknown ocean for his king [**doc. 31**]. Four years later, Pedrarias, governor of Darien, moved the seat of his administration from Nombre de Dios on the Caribbean side of the isthmus to Panama on the Pacific side, his main object being to continue the search for a strait between the two oceans. Gradually the coastlines north of Panama – Veragua, Costa Rica, Honduras – were explored by ships from Panama, although no strait was found. To the south the coast was barren and forbidding, similar to the African coast explored by Cão and Dias 40 years previously. Prevailing south-west winds and the cold and northwards-flowing Humboldt current also made exploration difficult.

It was not until 1526 that the existence of another great inland empire, on a similar scale to that of Mexico, was suspected. In that year ships under Bartholomew Ruiz encountered an ocean-going balsa raft not far north of the equator. It had fine cotton sails and carried gold and silver ornaments, clearly products of an advanced culture.

The following year, Francisco Pizarro, on his second expedition, arrived at the Indian city of Túmbes. He saw well-planned streets with stone public buildings, and he met an Inca nobleman who wore gold ear plugs and a llama wool cloak slung over one shoulder like a Roman senator.

Pizarro was a tough, illiterate *hidalgo* in his fifties, very different from the well-educated Cortés with whom history has bracketed him. He was to display qualities of enterprise, endurance and tenacity equal to those of Cortés, but he lacked the latter's psychological subtlety or his administrative ability (**26, 41, 45**).

In 1528 Pizarro returned to Spain from the New World, taking with him samples of Peruvian gold and silver work and finely woven cloth. Charles V was impressed enough to appoint him governor of the new colony he intended to conquer. In 1531 he was ready to set sail again from Panama, with three ships, 180 men and 27 horses.

Pizarro's luck was phenomenal. If he had tried to conquer Peru at any other time – on the occasion of the earlier expedition, for instance – he would have failed. But at the moment of his arrival the Inca empire was split in two. Huáyna Capac, the 'Inca', had died in 1527 and his two sons, Atahualpa and Huáscar, had fought a brutal civil war for the succession. Huáscar, the younger of the two, was the legitimate heir, but Atahualpa had been with his father on a campaign in the northern region round Quito and had the support of the veteran Inca captains. Just before his meeting with Pizarro, Atahualpa captured Huáscar in a major battle near Cuzco.

The Inca was even more absolute a ruler than the Aztec emperor, and his authority more unquestioned than that of any contemporary European monarch. Atahualpa's family were said to be descended from the sun and his slightest word was law across the 5,000 kilometres of Inca territory. Elaborate rituals surrounded his daily life; for instance, everything he touched, such as clothes or dishes, had to be carefully preserved and later ceremonially burnt.

Under the Inca the empire was ruled by a highly privileged class of nobles who enjoyed special food, clothing, and even the exclusive use of certain roads and bridges forbidden to the common people. The foundation of this administratively sophisticated empire rested on the docile, fatalistic and obedient Peruvian peasants. In their thousands they had built the great military highways, constructed the walls and palaces with masonry so precise that it seemed there was no room for mortar between the stones, hewed the irrigation channels on the coastal plain, and, in the mountains, the elaborate stone terraces for agriculture. Like the Aztecs the Incas knew neither the wheel nor writing, but they did have the llama for wool and transport. Their empire was far more of an administrative unit than the loose federation of peoples that the Aztecs dominated.

Soon after his arrival at Túmbes, Pizarro heard that Atahualpa and his army were at Cajamarca some 640 kilometres away, and 3,000 metres up in the High Andes. We know less about the Spaniards' subsequent movements and motives than we do about those of Cortés because there was no Bernal Diaz to chronicle them, but it seems clear that Pizarro, who naturally knew Cortés's story, decided to try and emulate him by taking the Inca prisoner. However, when he arrived on the heights overlooking Cajamarca and saw Atahualpa's army encamped, even Pizarro must have been seized with apprehension about his own position. His little force was weeks away from possible reinforcements and he was now in contact with a victorious and disciplined army of perhaps 80,000 soldiers.

Atahualpa, for his part, completely underestimated the Spanish. He let them march through the mountains to his position, when he could easily have had them ambushed as they scaled the heights. Most probably he regarded them as a curiosity rather than as any conceivable threat. When they appeared he received them politely, giving them for their quarters the stone-built and easily defensible settlement of Cajamarca which was a kilometre or two away from his encampment and which he emptied of its inhabitants for their benefit. On the evening the Spaniards arrived Atahualpa accepted an invitation from Pizarro to visit him the following day, and this he duly did, unaccountably deciding to enter the square of Cajamarca with only some 5,000 of his men, and these unarmed. Clearly it never occurred to him that the Spaniards, situated as they were, would dare to attack him without provocation or warning. But this is precisely what they did. It was the most decisive event in the history of the conquests, one which the Spaniards had thoroughly rehearsed and which went according to plan [**doc. 32**]. When Atahualpa entered the square, carried on a litter and surrounded by sumptuously decked-out nobles, he was approached by a Spanish priest who harangued him on the subject of Christianity. Atahualpa, predictably, threw the bible which had been put into his hand on to the ground. On this pretext Pizarro gave the pre-arranged signal, a dropped handkerchief, the Spanish cannon opened up and the cavalry dashed out from their concealment. For two hours the Spaniards massacred those who failed to escape through the two small exits to the square. Atahualpa's nobles died to a man, trying to protect him with their bare hands. The only wound sustained by a Spaniard was when Pizarro cut his hand while trying to restrain his bloodthirsty followers from finishing the ruler off. Atahualpa spent the brief remainder of his life a captive. The Inca army encamped nearby seemed stunned when shorn of its leader, and the warriors melted away back to their homes. Pizarro had achieved his wildest dreams by a stroke of fortune. The great Inca empire, still hardly penetrated, let alone explored, had been conquered. The Europeans' first glimpse of Inca majesty coincided with its overthrow.

As had happened in Mexico, the Inca continued to function as an absolute ruler when in captivity. Atahualpa was even more abject and anxious to please than Montezuma had been. He soon made his famous offer: in exchange for his freedom, his subjects would undertake within two months to fill with gold a room measuring about 7 by 5 by 2.5 metres [**doc. 33**]. Atahualpa may have been playing for time, hoping that the Spaniards would go away, or that he might escape, but he does not seem to have doubted that they would keep their word if he kept his. Pizarro also needed time – to send back to Panama for reinforcements; in any case it made his task of looting the Inca empire much easier if the gold was collected for him. During the following weeks sheets of beaten gold torn from temple walls and gold ornaments of enormous value were brought into Cajamarca, by llama or on native backs. Atahualpa gave no orders to his generals to oppose the Spaniards. His only independent action was secretly to order the death of his brother, Huáscar, still in captivity. This was to forestall the possibility of Pizarro using him as an alternative figurehead.

When most of the gold promised had been collected it was melted down, as in Mexico, so that the king of Spain, the leaders and their followers, could receive their share. In the spring the awaited reinforcements arrived, led by Diego de Almagro, an old comrade-in-arms of Pizarro. In July, rumours, later proved false, of a planned Indian rising gave the Spaniards the excuse needed to eliminate Atahualpa, who had by now served his purpose. A travesty of a trial was held and he was found guilty on various counts including the worship of idols. He was sentenced to be burnt, and the sentence was only commuted to garotting after he had allegedly begged, and received, baptism. According to Inca religion a body destroyed by fire was not eligible for the after-life. The news of this crime startled Europe and was condemned by Charles V himself.

Now Pizarro was ready to leave Cajamarca and march on the

Inca capital, Cuzco. The march and entry into the capital were not unopposed, but the Spaniards had the advantage that a large part of the population had supported Huáscar and therefore saw them as liberators against Atahualpa, another parallel with the earlier situation in Mexico. Atahualpa was followed by a series of compliant puppet Incas whom the Spanish used to control the government on their behalf. However, one of these, Manca, later led the great rebellion of 1536, which came close to capturing the capital. This episode was brought about by the Spaniards' greed and administrative incompetence. In the period after the conquest they took the gold and silver and divided up the land between themselves, but neglected to maintain the irrigation channels and wilfully slaughtered herds of llamas. However, Manca's revolt was doomed to failure. Even if he had killed all the Spaniards in Peru – and he did in fact kill a third of them – he was really pitting himself against the resources of a world-wide empire, and when reinforcements arrived from other parts of the New World, and from Spain, the revolt was over.

Why did these empires fall so easily to the Spaniards? Both the Aztecs and the Incas were familiar with organised war and had large numbers of men trained and under arms. Their weapons were by no means negligible; the Aztec axe, with its obsidian blade, could cut off a horse's head; the Incas possessed bronze spears and shields. Partly, it was due to a characteristic they shared. Their considerable degree of cultural, artistic and political development was combined with technological weakness when compared with Europe. They had no written alphabet, no iron, no wheeled vehicles, no ships except the most rudimentary, few domestic beasts of burden, and not even the plough. Another characteristic they shared was a high level of social conformity and docility. Without the subservience of the individual to the state such impressive empires could hardly have arisen, given their primitive technology. Inca irrigation, in particular, needed large-scale collective labour. Their system of rule, centred on semi-divine emperors and small elites of nobles, tended to produce passive obedience rather than active loyalty. These political systems were especially vulnerable to an enemy with technical superiority and mobility, who could reach and seize the centres of power.

The conquistadors had such superiority. As well as cannon and musket – neither of which played a vital part in the conquests, though they were no doubt terrifying and contributed to the Spaniards' god-like image – they had the great advantage of steel over bronze or stone. The Indians had no answer to razor-sharp Toledo steel blades, handled by experienced swordsmen. The Spaniards also possessed horses, although not many – Cortés had only 16 when he landed in Mexico. Even more important were factors of motivation and temperament. The conquistadors were tough individualists from the harsh uplands of Castile. The narrative of the conquest brings out the three strands in their psychology: a wolfish greed for gold; a passionate longing to strike down the heathen and win souls for Christ; a chivalric love of great deeds for their own sake (**37**).

Other factors were that, in the case of both Mexico and Peru, the Spaniards were able to exploit the legends and superstitions of the enemy so as to weaken opposition, at least temporarily. Again, the Aztec preoccupation with taking prisoners for sacrifice rather than killing them put them at a disadvantage in battle. More important was the disunity of which the Spaniards took full advantage: in Mexico between the Aztecs and their subservient peoples, especially the Tlaxcalans; in Peru between the followers of Atahualpa and Huáscar. Finally, the fatalism of both Aztec and Inca religion could not stand up to the truculent confidence of Renaissance Christianity. In the Old World this had been less of an advantage because the enemy was usually Moslem, an equally optimistic faith, with similar attitudes towards war and death. But, as J. H. Parry puts it, 'Amerindian religion . . . was profoundly pessimistic, the sad, acquiescent faith of the last great Stone Age culture. The Indian believed that his religion required him to fight, and if need be, to die bravely. The Spaniard believed that his religion enabled him to win' (**54**).

The rule of the conquistadors was quarrelsome and brief. By 1550 they had been largely supplanted by a bureaucracy of officials, lawyers and priests sent out from Spain to govern the new lands. The process took longer in Peru than in Mexico, where Cortés enjoyed a unique prestige so that there was no other conquistador faction to challenge him. But even Cortés was not fully trusted, precisely because he had such prestige.

In 1528 he returned to Spain and met Charles V who greeted him warmly and confirmed the vast *encomienda* he had granted to himself, of over 23,000 Indian families. Nevertheless, Charles sent out a viceroy and an *audiencia*, or committee of lawyers, to govern Mexico. In 1539 Cortés finally retired to Spain, a disillusioned man. During the last years of his life his house in Madrid became the centre for a circle of humanist intellectuals including John Dantiscus, the Polish ambassador to the Imperial Court and a friend of Copernicus. These humanists did much, after Cortés's death in 1539, to perpetuate his fame and his ideas.

In Peru bureaucratic rule was held up by civil wars between factions of the victorious conquistadors. The first of these, the war of Las Salinas, ended with the defeat of Almagro by the Pizarro brothers in 1538. Three years later Francisco Pizarro was murdered by supporters of the late Almagro, and a second struggle, the war of Chupas, broke out. In 1546 there was more violence – a rising of the settlers led by Gonzalo Pizarro, the last of the five brothers, against an incompetent viceroy from Spain who tried to enforce the New Laws. Not until 1548 was the fighting finally concluded.

By mid-century both Mexico and Peru were relatively peaceful and starting to prosper. Cities had sprung up, either newly sited – as at Lima, which the Spaniards built as a more suitable capital for Peru than the mountainous Cuzco – or on old Indian sites. Mexico City was the largest settlement in the New World. By 1550 it may have had nearly 100,000 inhabitants, larger than Santo Domingo and far out-distancing any city in Spain. New World cities were independently run by self-perpetuating but civic-conscious *cabíldos*, or councils, and were often well planned, with elegant churches and public buildings. Charles V tended to favour municipal self-government, and there was some chance during his reign that the *cabíldos* would increase in influence. There was talk of setting up a colonial Cortes (Parliament) like that of Castile. However, centralising tendencies eventually took over, and the power of the cities declined relative to that of the bureaucracy (**47**).

In the countryside the *encomienda*, as started by Columbus and Cortés in order to reward their own followers, remained the basic agricultural unit. But by mid-century the *encomienda* had been modified to some degree in the interests of the Indians by Spanish legislation, in particular the Code of 1542 known as the New Laws.

In 1545 the rich silver mines at Potosí in Peru (modern Bolivia) were opened up. The discovery of this mountain of silver has been called one of the turning points in the history of the western world (**30**). The ensuing silver rush turned Potosí into a vast shanty town, even though the mines lay at 18,000 metres, a dangerous altitude for heavy manual labour. Silver was mined in Mexico as well as Peru, and gold also, though in much smaller quantities; by now the gold-bearing rivers of Hispaniola had been exhausted. The main export to Europe next to silver was cochineal, the tiny red beetle parasitic on cactus, which when crushed yielded a valuable dye.

By this time, too, the New World was producing its own food, including wheat, grapes and olives, and the import of bulk foodstuffs from Spain was becoming uneconomic. The rearing of cattle and sheep, both introduced from Spain, was a highly successful activity, especially in Mexico, where beef became so cheap that carcasses were often left to rot once the hide and the fat, for tallow, had been removed. In spite of this self-sufficiency, trade between Seville and the New World had steadily increased, and in exchange for silver came books, textiles, weapons, and other products of Old World civilization, as well as fresh supplies of manpower. In 1550, 133 ships crossed the Atlantic west-bound, and 82 east-bound (**55**).

5 England and France

John Cabot

Early exploration of the North Atlantic coasts of America, in which England played the major role, took place during the same period that Columbus was exploring the Caribbean, and the Portuguese were penetrating to the Far East. Unfortunately, however, much less is known of this aspect of the discoveries. There are no first-hand accounts of voyages by those who took part in them and we have to rely on indirect sources such as ambassadors' reports, the wording of royal patents, or entries in official records showing that a certain explorer had been rewarded with a pension (**50,61,66**).

England's role is associated with John Cabot, a much-travelled Genoese or possibly a Venetian, who appeared in Bristol in about 1495, and also, later, with his son, Sebastian. John Cabot's achievements are far less well documented than those of Columbus or da Gama and even the dates of his voyages are still debated. An additional factor which has tended until quite recently to obscure John Cabot's reputation is that his better-known son seems to have done little to preserve his father's fame. Until the end of the nineteenth century historians mistakenly thought that it was Sebastian, and not John, who led the expedition of 1497 to Newfoundland.

John Cabot may have come to England because it occurred to him that England was at the end of the spice line and paid the highest prices, and therefore that a radical proposal to search for a new spice route would be welcomed there most of all. It was also natural that he should come to Bristol, which faced the Atlantic and which had been, since 1400, the second seaport in the country. Bristol was to have, through the Cabots, a distinguished record in the period of European expansion (**80**).

On his arrival Cabot, with his Renaissance horizons, must have impressed the somewhat insular merchants of Bristol. Before this date very few people in England had heard of Cathay or Cipango or the current search for new routes to them (**89**). There were no English translations of D'Ailly or Marco Polo until the turn of the century. Spices for sale in England were brought annually to Southampton in the great galley fleet from Venice. Bristol merchants would have been excited by Cabot's proposal to find a new route to the source of the spices, because it promised, if successful, to make Bristol rather than Southampton the centre for this most lucrative of all trades.

English seamen were, on the other hand, already familiar with the Atlantic ocean as a trade highway. By 1490 there was a regular trade between England and the islands of the South Atlantic – Madeira, the Canaries and probably the Azores. Bristol merchants had also traded with Iceland since at least the early fifteenth century. There is evidence of a small group of Bristol merchants who traded extensively with both Iceland and Portugal in the 1480s. They sold Icelandic cod to the Portuguese, though the Icelandic fisheries declined towards the end of the century. This in turn may have meant that English seamen had heard about the lands to the west which Icelandic ships visited. Both Iceland and Norway supported colonies in Greenland during the Middle Ages and modern archaeology has shown that at least one of these colonies survived until the early sixteenth century (**66**). Moreover, Icelandic sagas told of lands even further to the west – Helluland, Markland and Vinland. The two former may have been on the coast of Labrador or Newfoundland, Vinland further to the south. Was it coincidence that John Cabot's 1497 landfall in Newfoundland was very likely within a few miles of the site where Leif Ericson tried to found a colony in 1001? It probably was coincidence; nevertheless it seems quite likely that rumours of these western lands, with their timber and their cod, were current in England before Cabot's arrival.

References in official documents show that at least two voyages of discovery set out from Bristol in the 1480s to look for the 'island of Brazil'. The clearest evidence for this comes from documents relating to an enquiry held about evasion of customs duties by a certain ship's captain, Thomas Croft. The jury exonerated Croft on the grounds that his ship and goods were not to be used for trade but 'to search out and discover a certain island called the Isle of Brazil' (**61**). Where 'Brazil' was supposed to be and whether it was ever reached is conjectural, but it may well have been on the North American mainland, perhaps on the same latitude as Bristol, perhaps even the Vinland of the sagas.

Between these 'Brazil' voyages and 1496, when John Cabot was given his first patent by Henry VII, the king had received two important visitors, either of whom might have brought him up to date with the latest ideas on the western Atlantic and a possible route to Asia. In 1489 Bartholemew Columbus, Christopher's younger brother, came to England to try and obtain royal support for a voyage to Asia, an attempt which failed. And in 1493 another geographical expert also visited England, although unwillingly. This was Martin Beheim, a German in the service of John II of Portugal. The previous year he had constructed a famous globe which incorporated the Columbus-Toscanelli view about the nearness of Cathay. Beheim was sent by John to the Netherlands, probably in connection with intrigues over the Yorkist pretender, Perkin Warbeck, but he was captured at sea and taken to England where he spent three months in custody before release (**61, 62, 74**). Information retailed by either of these visitors might have given Henry VII's advisers enough confidence in the prospects of western exploration to lead them to support the ideas of Cabot.

John Cabot had read his Marco Polo and had the same ambition as Columbus, to reach Asia by a western route. This is clear from the reports about his 1497 voyage, in particular that by the Milanese ambassador, Soncino, in a letter to his master, Duke Ludovico Sforza [**doc. 37**]. The wording of the patent Cabot received from Henry also gives the impression that Cabot himself did not believe that Columbus had reached Asia. The patent permits Cabot to take ships of any tonnage he chose, to sail to any part of the 'eastern, western and northern sea', in order to investigate 'whatsoever islands, continents, regions or provinces of heathens or infidels, in whatsoever part of the world placed, which before this time were unknown to Christians'. The implication here, according to the late J. A. Williamson, who was the foremost authority on Cabot, is that Henry was prepared to respect the Spaniards' settlement in Hispaniola, and even their right to a monopoly of the sea-route that led to it, and told Cabot that he must not sail to the 'southern' sea, i.e. he should keep to the latitude of England in crossing the Atlantic (**66**). However, Henry was not prepared to recognise the claims of the Treaty of Tordesillas. He might have missed the opportunity to sponsor Columbus himself, but this made him even more determined to prevent Spain and Portugal monopolising future New World discoveries (**82**). So Cabot, once across the Atlantic, was to be allowed to investigate *all* lands. He was expected to reach Asia by a northerly route and then follow the Asiatic coast southwards until he came to Cathay. In so doing he would have sailed right round Hispaniola, leaving the Spanish marooned, so to speak, only half way to their goal. The patent goes on to repeat the formula which was by now becoming standard, that newly discovered lands were to be occupied in the name of the king, and that one fifth of all profits from the voyage were to go to the royal purse.

Until recently historians thought that Cabot's first voyage, for which this was the patent, took place in 1497, but an important and recently discovered letter from John Day, an English merchant in Spain, seems to indicate an earlier voyage, in 1496 (**50, 66**) [**doc. 38**]. The letter is addressed to the 'Lord Grand Admiral', who is almost certainly Columbus. Although undated, internal evidence suggests it was written between December 1497 and early 1498, which would have been too early for news of the 1497 voyage. At this time Columbus was probably systematically reassessing his own original project of a western route to Asia. He had returned from his second voyage in 1496 and could not have been altogether happy with the discoveries he had so far made. He would have been intensely interested in any information obtainable from rival explorers.

Nothing is known of Cabot's 1496 voyage, which presumably failed, but that of 1497 is better documented. It was made in a very small ship, the *Mathew*, a vessel similar to Columbus's *Niña*, with a crew of 18. Cabot sailed westward on a northerly latitude, and made landfall somewhere on the present American or Canadian coast. Precisely where has been the subject of enormous speculation. The controversy has been fuelled by national sentiment in that certain English and Canadian historians have been anxious to show that Cabot reached the mainland before Columbus did, in 1498.

Two possibilities canvassed for Cabot's landing have been Cape Race, the southern tip of Newfoundland, and Cape Breton Island, off Nova Scotia. It is also possible that he reached the coast of Maine. One piece of alleged evidence which has complicated the argument is the '1500' world map of the Spanish cartographer, Juan de la Cosa. When discovered in a Paris antique shop in 1833 this produced a sensation because it shows a series of English flags planted along an American coastline which appears to stretch from Labrador to Florida. Along with the flags there is an inscription, 'sea discovered by an Englishman'. It may be that Columbus sent on to la Cosa the rough sketchmap which accompanied John Day's letter to him [**doc. 38**] and which was itself copied from a sketch made by Cabot during the voyage. However, la Cosa's map is now almost illegible, and the American part of it may be considerably later than 1500, which would lessen its likely connection with Cabot (**50, 72**).

The most plausible hypothesis as to where Cabot went in 1497 goes as follows (**66**). He sailed from Bristol to Ireland and then steered due west on latitude 51 degrees from Dursey Head, north of Bantry Bay. Some 32 days later he sighted land near Cape Dégrat, the north-easternmost point of Newfoundland. Like all the early navigators his technique would have been to find a suitable latitude and then stick to it until he made landfall. He proceeded to skirt the coast southwards, looking for a suitable place to land, which he did, ceremoniously taking possession of the territory in the names of Henry VII, the Pope and Venice. He then sailed along the entire coast of Newfoundland until it trended sharply westwards after Cape Race. Deciding to leave further exploration until the following year he then returned to his original landfall, Cape Dégrat, before sailing back across the Atlantic. We know that on the return journey he reached Brittany in the impressive time of 15 days, an average speed of five knots, not impossible given the strong westerly winds prevalent in that latitude. He arrived back in Bristol on 6 August 1497, and within a few days was in London apprising Henry of his success. He himself, and no doubt others, believed that he had reached Asia. As Soncino wrote home to Milan, 'His Majesty here has gained part of Asia without a stroke of the sword' [**doc. 37**].

In spite of the fact that this was a difficult time politically for the king – it was the year of the Cornish rebellion against war taxation levied to provide an army to deal with Perkin Warbeck – Henry treated Cabot generously. The royal household books show him receiving not only an immediate reward of £10 but also an annuity of £20 payable from the Bristol customs. This, however, he did not survive long to enjoy. The following summer he was off again. Little is known about the 1498 voyage except that there were five ships, four supplied and equipped by Bristol merchants and one by the king. This seems an insignificant fleet compared with the 17 ships taken by Columbus on his second voyage, or the 13 Vasco da Gama took on his. It may reflect not only the state of Henry's exchequer as compared with those of the Spanish and Portuguese sovereigns, but also some lack of confidence about Cabot's discoveries of 1497. The '98 expedition was clearly seen by the king as an outside gamble – a chance, not a certainty, of rich profits. Soon after the voyage started one of the ships was damaged and put back to an Irish harbour, and the others, including Cabot's, disappeared. However, there is a shred of circumstantial evidence which indicates that

Cabot might have explored the whole North American coastline on this voyage, down to the Caribbean, and that some part of the fleet returned to tell the tale. This is Williamson's view, and the main evidence he adduces is the patent granted to a Spanish captain, Alonso de Hojeda, in 1501. Hojeda was authorised to proceed to the Venezuela region and there 'to follow that coast which you have discovered, which runs east and west, as it appears, because it goes towards the region where it has been learnt that the English were making discoveries; and that you go setting up marks with the arms of their Majesties . . . so that you may stop the exploration of the English in that direction' (**66**).

'Labrador'

Between 1499 and 1505 there were several other voyages to the north-west Atlantic by both Portuguese and English explorers (**50, 61**). There is also evidence of collaboration between the two nations. The Portuguese had long been active in the Atlantic, and half a century earlier had founded and colonised the Azores. In 1499 an Azorean 'Labrador' (farmer) named Juan Fernandez received a patent for exploration from the king of Portugal. The following year a nobleman from the Azores, Gaspar Corte Real, received another patent and made a voyage northwards. He sighted, but did not land on, Cape Farewell, the southernmost tip of Greenland. By this time the Norse colonies in Greenland had either been abandoned or at least become isolated from Europe (**66**), so that Corte Real in effect re-discovered the country. It is not known whether Fernandez accompanied Corte Real, but in 1501 the former turned up in England and imparted news of this discovery. Because of this Greenland became known as the land of the Labrador, although later on the name Labrador was transferred to North America. Fernandez took service in England, and in 1501 Letters Patent were issued to him and two other Portuguese, together with three Bristol merchants, to explore and annex 'heathen lands hitherto unknown to all Christians'. This meant that they were debarred both from Greenland and also from the coasts discovered by Cabot, whose patent was not cancelled. It seems likely that the new syndicate was expected to explore northwards between Newfoundland and Greenland. The implication is that by now the search was on for a north-west passage, a way to Asia round the intervening landmass of North America.

Gaspar Corte Real made another voyage in 1501. He went to

Greenland, then turned west and coasted the length of Newfoundland and along Labrador. He sent home two of his ships but subsequently disappeared in the third. In 1502 his brother Miguel sailed to the same region, and he also disappeared with his ships. The motives of these voyages are unknown, but are again likely to have included a search for a passage to Asia. Vasco da Gama had taken two years to reach India and return, and a shorter route was obviously worth looking for.

Evidence from patents and from the monetary rewards granted to explorers proves that English voyages were also made regularly until 1505, and that something considered of benefit was discovered. In 1502 Henry VII issued a new patent of a different kind. The grantees were empowered to 'recover' any heathen lands in any part of the world, and it was no longer stipulated that such lands must hitherto have been unknown to Christians. The only limitation was that the lands must not be now in the *possession* of Christians. This was the doctrine of effective occupation which was to be invoked 80 years later by Elizabeth when she dispatched Raleigh to found a colony in Virginia. The wording of the 1502 patent, and its elaborate clauses about setting up a government, show that permanent colonies were also in contemplation at this date. It is quite possible in fact that a colony was founded which has left no historical traces. Nor do we know where these expeditions went. One possible indication is that in 1505 'Popyngais and cattes of the montaign' were brought back to England from some voyage. According to D. B. Quinn this suggests penetration as far south as the present boundary of the USA and Canada, since neither parrots nor lynxes were ever indigenous any further north (**61**).

Sebastian Cabot

The contribution of Sebastian Cabot to this sequence of voyages is not yet clear. Nineteenth-century historians such as the American Henry Harisse found no evidence that he had been involved in any voyages at all at this time, but later research proved that he made an expedition to high latitudes in 1508–9. More recently the correct version of a grant made to him by Henry VII in 1505 has been unearthed, and this proves that he also made a voyage in 1504 to the 'newe founde lande' (**91**). This voyage involved two ships, the *Jesus* and the *Gabriel*, setting sail from Bristol, fitted out by Bristol merchants, Robert Thorne and Hugh Elyot. The ships returned with cargoes of fish, but, apart from the phrase in the grant, 'the fyndynge of the newe founde landes', there is no evidence as to their destination.

Sebastian Cabot set out again in the last year of Henry VII's reign. There are no eye-witness accounts of this voyage either, but from later sources it appears that he sailed to the Labrador coast, and perhaps as far north as Baffin Island. He then skirted the east coast of North America, probing for a north-west passage. It is not known how far south he got; one source says to the latitude of Cuba. He may have ceased exploration because he realised that he was entering the Spanish sphere of influence. He returned home, presumably by way of the gulf stream and the Westerlies, possibly the first English explorer to take such a southerly route (**50**).

If this account of Sebastian Cabot's 1508–9 voyage is correct, he must have put England in the lead so far as knowledge of the North American coastline was concerned. However, he had failed to find a passage to Asia and this may account for the lack of follow-up to the voyage. The possibility of finding such a route must by now have seemed increasingly remote to those who knew what the Portuguese were doing, and were soon to hear of Magellan's feat. And Henry VIII, the young monarch who was on the throne when Cabot returned in 1509, was clearly interested in more exciting, continental projects rather than in carrying on a series of barren explorations, which were also expensive in lives and ships. Moreover he was married to a Spaniard and perhaps disliked the idea of appearing to interfere with Spanish interests in the New World.

In 1512 Sebastian Cabot left England for Spain, where he spent the next 30 years as an important official, becoming in 1518 chief pilot of the *Casa de Contratación* at Seville, the post originally held by Vespucci. In 1548 he returned to England where he spent the last decade of his life. During this time he was an influential adviser to both Somerset and Northumberland, and later to the Marian Privy Council. In 1550 the English cloth trade had collapsed and London merchants were ready to consider projects for establishing new trade routes. Cabot's expertise was undoubtedly useful in planning voyages to the Levant and the Barbary coast in 1551, and above all in the preparations for the expedition of Willoughby and Chancellor to Russia in 1553. He was made governor for life of the Muscovy Company which was set up after Chancellor's return from Moscow in 1554, but died three years later.

Sebastian Cabot's main achievement, so far as we can tell, lies in his voyage of 1508–9, which charted the coast of North America. It is true that this voyage was to provide the rationale for a whole series of abortive attempts to find a north-west passage, over the next two centuries, but this hardly detracts from Cabot's achievement.

France

France entered the age of discoveries even later than England. Louis XI had been absorbed in the creation of a centralised monarchical state, an enterprise which led to a series of wars, first with neighbouring Burgundy and then against the Habsburgs. Thus energies which might have gone on voyaging were diverted to the battlefields of Italy and Savoy. Nevertheless, Francis I, who succeeded his cousin Louis XII in 1515, took a keen, though fitful, interest in discovery when more pressing demands such as successive rounds of war permitted. The story of the circumnavigation started by Magellan and completed by El Cano made a great impression on him and Antonio Pigafetta, Magellan's friend and the chronicler of the voyage, was invited to the French court in 1523. By now the entire American coastline from Florida to Patagonia had been explored, either by Spain or Portugal. It was clear that if a strait through to Asia existed it must be somewhere north of Florida (**42, 50**).

Verrazzano

Giovanni da Verrazzano, a Florentine nobleman who had connections with France, was chosen to lead an expedition (**25, 50**). The project was financed largely by a group of Florentine bankers operating in Lyons and Rouen. Verrazzano's ship, *La Dauphine*, recently built in the royal dockyard of Le Havre and named after the dauphin, Francis, was lent by the king. She was of 100 tonnes, approximately twice as large as John Cabot's *Mathew*, and carried a crew of 50. Verrazzano's objective was clear; as he subsequently wrote to the king: 'My intention on the voyage was to reach Cataia (Cathay) and the extreme eastern coast of Asia, not expecting to find such a barrier of new land as I did find, and, if I did find such land, I estimated that it would not lack a strait to penetrate to the Eastern Ocean' (**50**).

In January 1524, Verrazzano left Brittany, and sailed to Cape Fear in the Carolinas, having stopped off at Madeira *en route*. He then proceeded northwards along the Carolina Banks, a strip of sand less than a mile wide which separates the Atlantic from

Pamlico Sound and the real coastline of America. As he could not see the mainland from where he was, he concluded that the water which he could see on the other side of the Banks was the Pacific. This error was duly perpetuated by successive cartographers, who gave North America a narrow waist around North Carolina, and had the Pacific Ocean flowing over a large part of the area of the future United States.

Verrazzano continued northwards, missing the entrance to Chesapeake and Delaware Bays which he would presumably have explored as possible straits. He did enter New York Bay, his visit being now commemorated by the Verrazzano Bridge joining Staten Island with Long Island. Continuing east he traversed the coast of Maine and finally 'approached the land that in times past was discovered by the English, which is in 50°' (**25**). His latitude readings are usually accurate, so this presumably implies that he had covered most of the east coast of Newfoundland before turning for home, which he reached after a two-week crossing.

Verrazzano had discovered a continental landmass which clearly required further exploration, but his return coincided with a round of war, and a few months later Francis was captured at the battle of Pavia; thus it was not until 1527 that a second voyage set off. The fleet of four became separated in a gale and Verrazzano decided to cut his losses by felling a cargo of logwood in Brazil and returning to sell it to the clothiers of Rouen. A third voyage, in 1528, also took a southerly route, and Verrazzano's life ended when he waded ashore on an island – possibly Guadeloupe – and confronted a crowd of cannibalistic Caribs who cut up and ate his body while his brother looked on helpless from the safety of a boat.

Cartier

The next explorer to be patronised by Francis, Jacques Cartier, must be ranked as one of the most successful of the age (**41,42,50**). He made three voyages to unknown waters without losing a ship, and his exploration of the St Lawrence River provided the basis for the later French colonisation of Canada. Cartier's first voyage started in April 1534, when he left St Malo with three ships for northern waters to continue Verrazzano's search for a passage to Asia. He crossed the Atlantic to Newfoundland then sailed round Cape Dégrat, the northernmost tip of that island, and into the Gulf of St Lawrence, following the mountainous Labrador coast westwards. For a discoverer of new lands Cartier is refreshingly candid about his impression of this arid landscape, describing it as probably the land God gave to Cain.

Cartier made a complete circuit of the Gulf of St Lawrence. On the coast of Nova Scotia he made amicable contact with Indians, and especially with a Huron chief named Donnaconna who was so impressed that he allowed his two teenage sons to accompany the expedition back to France, on a promise of their eventual return. This voyage was probably seen by Cartier as a reconnaissance; he had not found a strait, but he knew where there was an opening to the west of the Gulf, and would return to explore it further.

Cartier's second voyage, of 1535, took him and his three ships again through the Strait of Bellisle into the Gulf of St Lawrence. He had left France in May, and by the end of August he was sailing up the St. Lawrence River. Close to modern Quebec he again met Donnaconna, whose sons were returned safely. After a pause at the Huron settlement he sailed further upstream in his smallest ship, leaving the others at Quebec. Not far from present-day Montreal even this pinnace had to be left behind and the expedition continued in ships' longboats. They reached Hochelaga, another much larger Huron settlement with fortifications and about 50 houses made of bark and wood. A little further up river they came upon the Lachine rapids, which have today been bypassed by a canal, but which then proved impassable. The Indians gave Cartier to understand that not far away to the west lay the kingdom of Saguenay, rich in gold and precious stones, but as he had already travelled nearly 1,600 kilometres from the Atlantic he decided to return home. It was late in the year when this decision was made, so they wintered near Quebec. From November to April the ships lay fast in the frozen river while the French subsisted largely on the generosity of the neighbouring Indian settlement, and not without losing several men from scurvy. Meanwhile, Donnaconna had been embroidering his story of the fabulous kingdom to the west where, he claimed, rubies could be picked up off the ground and the people were dressed in woollen cloth and were as white as the French. His imaginative lies proved his undoing because Cartier decided to kidnap him so as to present Francis I with incontrovertible evidence as to the need for a third voyage [**doc. 39**]. In May 1536 Cartier set sail for France, having press-ganged ten Indians, among them Donnaconna and his two sons. So ended the second, and most productive, of Cartier's voyages. He had opened up the greatest waterway for the future penetration of the new continent, and had formed some estimate of the natural and human resources of Canada, having established, in spite of the final kidnapping, a reasonable relationship with the Huron tribe – whom, incidentally, the French never referred to by Columbus's term of Indian, preferring to call them *sauvages* or *peaux-rouges* (red-skins).

For four years, until his death in 1540, the Huron chief, Donnaconna, acted as a publicity agent for the entirely mythical kingdom of Saguenay, embellishing his yarns for the delectation of the French court. Francis I was able to use the reports of this kingdom to set against the tangible achievements in the New World of his rival, Charles V. Here was another great empire, a rival to Mexico and Peru, waiting to be conquered by the French. Donnaconna even obligingly added cloves and pepper to the list of commodities obtainable in Saguenay. Thus a third voyage was necessary, this time with little prospect of getting through to China, but with the aim of colonisation and conquest. Preparations were delayed by yet another round of Habsburg-Valois war, which ended with the Treaty of Nice in 1538. Even after this there were interminable arguments about arrangements, particularly over the leadership. Eventually, for reasons unknown, Francis placed Cartier under the command of a protestant nobleman, the Sieur de Roberval, whose royal commission of 1541 gave him viceregal powers over the new lands. Meanwhile, Habsburg agents in France were sending back worrying reports about the scale of the new venture. To one Spaniard who remonstrated, citing the Treaty of Tordesillas, Francis is supposed to have made his famous reply that the sun shone for him as for others, and he would like very much to see Adam's will to learn how he divided up the world (**50**).

Cartier set out in May 1541, this time with five ships. Roberval said that he was not yet ready, but would follow shortly. The squadron sailed directly to the St Lawrence and Cartier left his ships at anchor near Quebec while he proceeded in two longboats. At a previously chosen site he founded a settlement which he called Charlesbourg-Royal after Charles, duc d'Orléans, son of the king. There they built a palisaded village, planted seeds of lettuce, cabbage and turnip and started collecting iron pyrites (which they hoped was gold) and quartz crystals ('diamonds'). From here Cartier made a final effort to find Saguenay but was again foiled by the series of rapids south-west of Montreal. We know little of what happened that winter, as the sole surviving account of the voyage, that of Hakluyt (**14**), breaks off after the return to Charlesbourg. Probably the new colony came under attack from the Indians, who would have resented any attempt at a permanent settlement, to say nothing of the previous abduction of their chief, who by this time had died in France. At any rate, Cartier raised camp in June 1542 and returned to Newfoundland. There in the harbour of St John's, a favourite rendezvous for French fishing boats, he met Roberval, whose departure from France had been delayed by financial problems. Roberval ordered Cartier to go back with him to the St Lawrence and explore further, but Cartier had had enough and returned to France where he passed the last 15 years of his life in honourable retirement. Roberval made his own search for Saguenay but eventually returned, equally unsuccessful.

For half a century the opportunities to create a French empire overseas which Verrazzano and Cartier had opened up were not exploited. Francis died in 1547 and his son and successor, Henry II, was uninterested in American exploration. During the second half of the century France was beset with religious wars and the only people leaving her shores were Huguenots fleeing from persecution. So it was not until the following century that the story of French exploration continued, with Samuel de Champlain.

Part Three: Assessment

To attempt even to summarise the results of the discoveries would be rash. One recent multi-volumed work has been devoted entirely to the effect that Asia had on Europe after da Gama brought the two together (**46**), and the implications for Europe of the discovery of the New World were surely even more far-reaching than the discovery of Asia. Again, the mid-sixteenth century is a purely arbitrary point at which to end an account of the discoveries. By 1550 Magellan's crew had circumnavigated the world, but Cavendish and Drake had not; the Caribbean had been colonised, but not Virginia; the Portuguese had reached India, but not the Dutch or the English.

The points that follow are therefore far from comprehensive. A good place to start might be to list some of the items which the New World presented to the Old. They include potatoes (by 1576 a hospital in Seville was feeding them to patients); tomatoes; cacao (from which the Aztecs had made a cold chocolate drink); tobacco (ironically first introduced for its alleged medicinal properties); maize; peanuts; turkeys; vanilla; rubber; kidney beans. Columbus's crew brought back hammocks from Hispaniola, and they soon became standard in European ships. Cortés's men exchanged diseases with the Indians, handing over smallpox and measles, and receiving syphilis and yaws. There were disastrous smallpox epidemics in Mexico in 1527, 1545 and 1575–76.

From Asia there was little entirely new because trade between Asia and Europe had persisted throughout the Middle Ages. All the spices brought home by Portuguese carracks, for instance, were already known. Apart from these, India's main contributions to Europe were rugs and carpets and cheaper textiles, many of the names of which stem from Indian places, such as calico (Calicut) and muslin (Mosul). The result was a minor revolution in European upper-class dress, involving the use for the first time of cotton underclothes and handkerchiefs.

Most European nations had gained small benefit from the discoveries by 1550. England and France had only the Newfoundland fishery and some small profits from privateering against the Spanish. Portugal had achieved a half-century of wealth and power through having reached the East first, but this was now coming to an end. The cost of her seaborne empire was crippling her, so that, by 1580, when Philip II succeeded the House of Avis, she was already in decline. German bankers, especially the Welsers and Fuggers of Augsburg, had invested substantially and profitably in New World ventures, as had Italians, but no German or Italian state had participated in the discoveries, although individual Italians played a prominent role.

However, the effects on one European nation were far-reaching. In 1550 the whole of the New World except the coast of Brazil belonged to Spain. One indisputable result of this was to increase the power and prestige of the Spanish crown. Great reserves of patronage were created by the absolute rights which the crown had in the new territories. Especially important was ecclesiastical patronage, since Pope Alexander VI had given this away to the Spanish monarchs in perpetuity. Charles kept the right to collect tithes and found new bishoprics. By the end of his reign there were 22 bishoprics and archbishoprics in the New World. He also controlled, through the bishops, the Inquisition which, unlike in Spain, had no separate existence from the diocesan organisation. In 1548, at Lima, was held the first *auto da fé* in the New World and on this auspicious occasion a Flemish pilot, Jan Millar, was burnt alive. There was too, all the prestige accruing from the vast missionary enterprise of converting the natives to Christianity. This went to Spain and not to the Pope. The fact that America was hardly mentioned at the Council of Trent shows that the papacy had effectively given up all rights in this area (**36**).

It has been suggested that the acquisition of such unrestrained power may have increased the authoritarian tendencies of the Spanish monarchy – a development reflected in the decline in the role of the *Cortes* of Castile during the sixteenth century. If so, an additional factor here may have been the export from Spain of potentially unruly elements of the population. About 200,000 people emigrated to the New World from Spain during the century. The history of the country might have been very different if tough characters like Cortés and Pizarro had remained in Spain all their lives. Richard Hakluyt certainly thought so, and looked forward to similar advantages for England when she acquired colonies.

America was not the first, or principal, factor in the creation of Spain's leading position in Europe; this had already been assured by her Italian successes at the beginning of the sixteenth century. However, the New World helped maintain Spain in this position until well into the seventeenth century. In terms of status the discoveries provided evidence that Charles V really was a world ruler, a worthy successor to Augustus and Charlemagne. Spanish conquests gave a new meaning to Charles's device of two columns, with the motto *Plus Oultre* (even further). Here was an empire which truly extended beyond the old bounds of the Pillars of Hercules (Gibraltar) (**67**). At the time of his abdication this empire was Charles's principal source of revenue, with territories vastly larger than all the rest of his dominions put together. During his reign there developed a complex system of colonial government to manage this empire. It was controlled from Spain by two institutions, the Council of the Indies and the *Casa de Contratación*. The Council had been run on an informal basis for many years by the powerful Bishop Fonseca, but on his death in 1524 the opportunity was taken to give it a definite legal existence. It had an all-embracing competence over appointments, correspondence and the enforcement of laws relating to the Indies. The *Casa de Contratación*, first established by Ferdinand and Isabella in 1503, remained permanently in Seville, controlling all exports and imports between Spain and the New World and all travel between them. During Charles's reign it developed a large bureaucracy, with its own criminal jurisdiction and prison, and a school of navigation for keeping maps and charts up to date and training pilots (**47**).

During the Habsburg-Valois wars, French corsairs operated in the Caribbean and Atlantic and it became necessary to protect the ships bringing back silver to Spain. A system of annual armed treasure fleets was started and a new tax, the *avería*, was imposed on all imports and exports to pay for this. Havana, which by the 1550s had taken over from Santo Domingo as the principal island port, was the rendezvous for ships from Nombre de Dios carrying Peruvian silver and for Mexican ships from Vera Cruz. Nombre de Dios also became an important entrepôt. Goods for Peru had to be trans-shipped there, ferried up the Sagres river and overland to Panama, and then re-shipped to Lima. Havana, Santo Domingo, Nombre de Dios, and the lesser ports such as Cartagena constantly petitioned Charles for better defences against incursion by privateers, but little was done until Philip II's reign.

In the New World itself a bureaucratic government developed, based on viceroys and *audiencias*, and controlled from Spain. Charles could not collaborate with men of the stamp of Cortés and the

Pizarro brothers 'any more than a bridge player whose methods are conservative, can be happy with a partner who is perpetually taking risks' (**47**). He had no intention of allowing America to become a collection of feudal apanages ruled by the heirs of those who had originally conquered it. The process of replacement had largely taken place by the end of the reign. By 1549 America was divided into seven provinces, each controlled by a viceroy and *audiencia*, or committee of lawyers. The most important of these were Lima and Mexico. The *audiencias* had the power to judge all officials, even including the viceroys, who nevertheless were extremely powerful, being the royal representatives on the spot.

Financially, it was only in his final decade as emperor that Charles really started to profit from America. The opening of the great silver mines at Potosi in 1545 was crucial. By 1554 the income from the New World was still only 12 per cent of total imperial revenue, but it was already vital because the annual arrival of the treasure fleet at Seville had become the security on which huge loans from Genoese bankers could be floated. By the end of Philip II's reign the American revenue was between a fifth and a quarter of the total. It enabled Philip to pursue his ambitious foreign policy – to retain the southern Netherlands, defeat the Turks at Lepanto, dispatch the Armada and intervene in France.

But in the long run the effect of the New World on Spain was debilitating. The backwardness of the Castilian economy prevented it from benefiting substantially from either the flood of new capital or the challenge of new markets. Instead, Castile gradually became a *rentier* economy, buying from abroad what it failed to manufacture at home. As a Venetian ambassador in the early seventeenth century remarked: 'The gold that comes from the Indies does on Spain as rain does on a roof – it pours on her and it flows away' (**31**). Much of it flowed into baroque art, and served to decorate the palaces and churches of Catholic Europe.

American gold was actually of far less significance than American silver. Between 1500 and 1650, 181 tonnes of gold and 16,000 tonnes of silver reached Europe officially from America, and further huge quantities came in by contraband (**36**). Contemporaries, and most historians, have been in no doubt that the silver was highly inflationary. However, the precise relationship between silver imports and commodity price rises in various countries is difficult to establish. One complication is that sixteenth-century inflation was certainly well under way throughout western Europe before the silver started to arrive. It can be said, at least, that the New World silver was a contributory cause of late sixteenth-century price rises, and that these affected Spain particularly badly because the Spanish commercial and industrial classes were too weak to take advantage of the opportunities created by inflation.

Though for Spain, as earlier for Portugal, the economic advantages of empire turned sour, this is not necessarily true for Europe as a whole. When Spain and Portugal were unable, or unwilling, to supply their colonies with the goods they needed, or to police the sea-routes adequately, French, English and Dutch interlopers appeared. During the seventeenth century Spain gradually lost her monopoly of the Caribbean and North America. If one takes a broad enough historical and geographical canvas, the effects of empire were beneficial. Such a viewpoint is developed in the thesis of the American historian Walter Prescott Webb, who saw Columbus's achievement as central to subsequent European progress. Webb argued that the discovery of America led to the opening of a new 'Great Frontier' for the 'Metropolis' (Europe). In 1500 Europe had a population of some 100 million occupying and exploiting 1,000 million hectares of land. The New World suddenly presented this population with another 5,000 million hectares of practically empty territory, thus creating an opportunity which launched Europe on four centuries of boom, a period ending only with the closure of the frontier in about 1900 (**44, 65**). This thesis, of course, leaves out of account all the other elements behind European development, from the Renaissance to the Industrial Revolution, but it provides a framework for discussion. Among recent historians who have followed up some of its implications have been, for instance, Pierre and Huguette Chaunu, who minutely investigated the statistics of trade between America and Seville over a century and a half. Their conclusion was that American needs stimulated the growth of a wide range of European industries, though not primarily Spanish ones (**30**).

Having looked at the effects of the discoveries on Europe, it might be fair to say a word about their effects on America. It has been estimated that 70 million people died as a result of the conquests, most of them in the sixteenth century (**30**). In the Caribbean the native population of entire islands was wiped out by a combination of overwork, disease and economic and cultural dislocation. As early as 1510 it was found necessary to ship in negro slaves from West Africa as a substitute form of labour. The slave trade, perhaps the most inhuman aspect of European history and one which was to last for three centuries, had begun.

Possibly many peasants in Mexico and Peru were not greatly affected at first by the substitution of a Spanish for an Aztec or Inca ruling elite, but even in these relatively developed regions the drop in population after the Spaniards came was startling. In Mexico it went down from 11 to $6\frac{1}{2}$ million in 21 years (1519–40). The wealth of America was plundered or squandered by Spaniards, who demolished Aztec cities, allowed Inca irrigation systems to fall into ruin, and destroyed herds of llama for sport. New kinds of farming were introduced, it is true, especially large-scale pastoral farming, but this often only made the Indians' lot worse. In the new colonial societies Indians, along with African slaves, invariably found themselves at the bottom of the social and economic structure, where they still are today. Would it be unfair to conclude that while America may have gained from her encounter with a more technologically advanced civilization, for contemporary Americans it was a disaster?

Most difficult to assess, but not for that reason any less important, are the effects of the discoveries on the consciousness of Europe. There were many who grasped the significance of the New World at an early stage. The verdict of the Portuguese chronicler Gomara, writing in 1552, is well known: 'The greatest event since the creation of the world (excluding the incarnation and death of Him who created it) is the discovery of the Indies'. Certain key accounts were widely circulated, such as Columbus's *First Letter*, which went into 20 editions by 1500. The first printed collection of documents relating to the voyages, Montalboddo's *Paesi novamente retrovati* (1507) went through 15 editions in four languages (**36**).

On the whole, however, the discoveries did not make as much impact on the educated public as might have been expected (**77**). Of books published in Portugal between 1540 and 1600, it has been estimated that 10 per cent at the most were concerned in any way with Asia, the focus of Portuguese activity (**88**). Nor was this particular to Portugal. In Europe as a whole, more concern was shown, for instance, about the threat of the Turks in Hungary than in any newly discovered land. Perhaps this was because the new lands were so unexpected and strange. It has been said that the attempt of one society to comprehend another inevitably forces it to reappraise itself, and this was no easy task for a Europe just emerging from its medieval strait-jacket. The very existence of America challenged old assumptions, and in particular it challenged the superiority of antiquity, on which both medieval and early Renaissance thought was based. Ptolemy had known nothing about

America, and had said that it was impossible to reach India by sea, so Ptolemy was wrong. The New World was full of new species of plants and animals unknown to ancient authorities including the great Aristotle. The Inca roads, the Aztec legal system, were clearly sophisticated products, yet they owed nothing to the example of Greece and Rome.

Facts like these must have led some people to a gradual realisation of the superiority of direct personal observation over reliance on traditional authority. 'Had I Ptolemy, Strabo, Pliny or Salinus here', wrote the Portuguese, Barros, 'I would put them to shame and confusion'. But it is important not to exaggerate. It would be historically naive, for instance, to see the discoveries as initiating a new mental outlook among European intellectuals which ultimately' led to the scientific breakthrough of the seventeenth century. The gap between the academic progress made during the century in maths and astronomy on the one hand and the achievements of the discoverers on the other was wide. The explorers were intrepid, but not necessarily open-minded. Readers at home were interested in the new lands, but they also wanted to hear if possible about the giants and monsters they had been brought up on, or about the Earthly Paradise where men still lived as they had in the Golden Age. Such preoccupations necessarily got in the way of objective appraisal. As J. R. Hale has said, 'Few of the meteorites of information from the discoverers entered the closed mental atmosphere of Europe without being burned out of shape'. It remains to be shown that any practical demands associated with the voyages provoked developments in scientific method or thought, and it is a fact that early modern science started in those nations least associated with the discoveries, such as England and Holland (**80**).

The existence of the Indians posed problems which greatly exercised the minds of sixteenth-century theologians. Where had they come from, and how was their geographical situation to be squared with Biblical accounts of the creation of man and his dispersal throughout the world after the flood? Also why had all these peoples been excluded for so long from the benefits of Christianity? And, to come to the present, how were they to be treated? The answer to the last question depended on the answers given to the other two. Some commentators explained the existence of America by referring to the myth of Atlantis, as developed by Plato and Seneca, thus neatly reconciling the New World with classical authority (**70**). Others looked to the Bible, to the lost ten tribes of Israel, or to the mysterious Ophir, land of gold and peacocks. As regards their treatment there was a major controversy between those such as the Dominicans, Montesinos and Las Casas, who wanted them treated as children of God, and those, particularly the Spanish settlers, who did not. In 1550 there occurred one of the most significant debates of the century, between Bartholemew de Las Casas, protector of the Indians, and Ginés de Sepúlveda, a Spanish humanist who held that they were naturally inferior and hence fit to be enslaved (**39**). The debate took place before 14 judges at Valladolid in Castile and lasted two months. Sepúlveda based his position on Aristotle and Aquinas as well as on the gospel text, 'Go out into the highways and hedges, and compel them to come in, that my house may be filled'. He maintained that this command justified war against the Indians in order to make them Christian. In the end this view was rejected, and Las Casas triumphed. According to the historian of this controversy, 'One more painful and faltering step was thus taken along the road of justice for all races' (**39**). One may doubt whether such debates led to much of a practical nature. The conditions of the Indians remained fairly intolerable. And even in the realm of ideas the urbane and tolerant view of a Montaigne, who argued that savage society was in certain respects superior to civilization, remained quite exceptional [**doc. 40**].

Part Four: Documents

Kinsai in the thirteenth century

Marco Polo's glowing description of cities in Cathay (China) such as Kinsai fired the imagination of fifteenth-century explorers including Columbus.

Along both sides of the main street, which runs, as we have said, from one end of the city to the other, are stately mansions with their gardens, and beside them the residences of artisans who work in their shops. Here at every hour of the day are crowds of people going to and fro on their own business, so that anyone seeing such a multitude would believe it a stark impossibility that food could be found to fill so many mouths. Nevertheless, every market day all these squares are thronged with a press of customers and traders bringing in supplies by cart and by boat, and the whole business is accomplished. Let me quote as an illustration the amount of pepper consumed in this city so that from this you may be able to infer the quantities of provisions – meat, wine, and groceries – that are required to meet the total consumption. According to the figures ascertained by Messer Marco from an official of the Great Khan's customs, the pepper consumed daily in the city of Kinsai for its own use amounts to 43 cart-loads, each cart-load consisting of 223 lb.

It was further stated in the report that the city was organized in twelve main guilds, one for each craft, not to speak of the many lesser ones. Each of these twelve guilds had 12,000 establishments, that is to say 12,000 workshops, each employing at least ten men and some as many as forty. I do not mean that they were all masters, but men working under the command of masters. All this work is needed because this city supplies many others of the province. As for the merchants, they are so many and so rich and handle such quantities of merchandise that no one could give a true account of the matter; it is so utterly beyond reckoning.

From *The Travels of Marco Polo*, trans. R. E. Latham, Penguin Books, 1958, p.188

Giants

The spurious Travels of Sir John Mandeville *was an immensely popular work of the fourteenth century, and was translated into all the chief European languages.*

And in those isles are many manners of folk of divers conditions. In one of them is a manner of folk of great stature, as they were giants, horrible and foul to the sight; and they have but one eye, and that is in midst the forehead. They eat raw flesh and raw fish. In another isle are foul men of figure without heads, and they have eyes in either shoulder one, and their mouths are round shaped like a horseshoe, y-midst their breasts. In another isle are men without heads; and their eyes and their mouths are behind in their shoulders. In another isle is a manner of folk that has a plat face, without nose or eyes; but they have two small holes instead of eyes, and they have a plat mouth, lipless. In another isle are foul men that have the overlip so great that, when they sleep in the sun, they cover all the visage with that lip. In another isle are folk of little stature, as they were dwarfs: and they are somewhat more than pigmies. They have no mouth, but they have instead of their mouth a little hole, and therefore, when they shall eat, them behoves suck it with a reed or a pipe. Tongues have they none; and therefore they speak not, but hiss and make signs as monkeys do, ilk one til other, and ilk one of them wots well what other means. In another isle are folk whose ears are so syde [long] that they hang down to the knees. In another isle are folk that have feet like horse, and on them they will run so swythe [swift] that they will overtake wild beasts and slay them to their meat through swiftness of foot. In another isle are folk which go on their hand and on their feet, as they were four-footed beasts; and they are rough and will climb into trees als lightly as they were apes. There is another isle where folk are that are both men and women, and have members of both the tane and the tother, and . . . when they use the member of men, they get childer; and when they use the member of women they bear childer. Another isle there is where the folk go on their knees wonderfully, and it seems as they should fall at ilk a pace; and they have on either foot eight toes. Yet is there another isle where the folk have but a [one] foot, and that foot is so broad that it will cover all the body and ombre [shade] it from the sun. And upon this foot will they run so fast that it is [wonder] to see.

From Mandeville's Travels, 2 vols., Hakluyt Society, 2nd Series, 1st vol., CI, 1950, p. 213 (**16**)

document 3

Prince Henry's motives

Azurara, a chronicler contemporary with Prince Henry (the Lord Infant), describes his motives for initiating the Portuguese voyages.

IN WHICH FIVE REASONS APPEAR WHY THE LORD INFANT WAS MOVED TO COMMAND THE SEARCH FOR THE LANDS OF GUINEA

We imagine that we know a matter when we are acquainted with the doer of it and the end for which he did it. And since in former chapters we have set forth the Lord Infant as the chief actor in these things, giving as clear an understanding of him as we could, it is meet that in this present chapter we should know his purpose in doing them. And you should note well that the noble spirit of this Prince, by a sort of natural constraint, was ever urging him both to begin and to carry out very great deeds. For which reason, after the taking of Ceuta he always kept ships well armed against the Infidel, both for war, and because he had also a wish to know the land that lay beyond the isles of Canary and that Cape called Bojador, for that up to his time, neither by writings, nor by the memory of man, was known with any certainty the nature of the land beyond that Cape. Some said indeed that Saint Brandan had passed that way; and there was another tale of two galleys rounding the Cape, which never returned. But this doth not appear at all likely to be true, for it is not to be presumed that if the said galleys went there, some other ships would not have endeavoured to learn what voyage they had made. And because the said Lord Infant wished to know the truth of this – since it seemed to him that if he or some other lord did not endeavour to gain that knowledge, no mariners or merchants would ever dare to attempt it – (for it is clear that none of them ever trouble themselves to sail to a place where there is not a sure and certain hope of profit – and seeing also that no other prince took any pains in this matter, he sent out his own ships against those parts, to have manifest certainty of them all. And to this he was stirred up by his zeal for the service of God and of the King Edward his Lord and brother, who then reigned.[1] And this was the first reason of his action.

The second reason was that if there chanced to be in those lands some population of Christians, or some havens, into which it would be possible to sail without peril, many kinds of merchandise might be brought to this realm, which would find a ready market, and reasonably so, because no other people of these parts traded with them, nor yet people of any other that were known; and also the products of this realm might be taken there, which traffic would bring great profit to our countrymen.

The third reason was that, as it was said that the power of the Moors in that land of Africa was very much greater than was commonly supposed, and that there were no Christians among them, nor any other race of men; and because every wise man is obliged by natural prudence to wish for a knowledge of the power of his enemy; therefore the said Lord Infant exerted himself to cause this to be fully discovered, and to make it known determinately how far the power of those infidels extended.

The fourth reason was because during the one and thirty years that he had warred against the Moors, he had never found a Christian king, nor a lord outside this land, who for the love of our Lord Jesus Christ would aid him in the said war. Therefore he sought to know if there were in those parts any Christian princes, in whom the charity and the love of Christ was so ingrained that they would aid him against those enemies of the faith.

The fifth reason was his great desire to make increase in the faith of our Lord Jesus Christ and to bring to him all the souls that should be saved – understanding that all the mystery of the Incarnation, Death, and Passion of our Lord Jesus Christ was for this sole end – namely the salvation of lost souls – whom the said Lord Infant by his travail and spending would fain bring into the true path. For he perceived that no better offering could be made unto the Lord than this; for if God promised to return one hundred goods for one, we may justly believe that for such great benefits, that is to say for so many souls as were saved by the efforts of this Lord, he will have so many hundreds of guerdons in the kingdom of God, by which his spirit may be glorified after this life in the celestial realm. For I that wrote this history saw so many men and women of those parts turned to the holy faith, that even if the Infant had been a heathen, their prayers would have been enough to have obtained his salvation. And not only did I see the first captives, but their children and grandchildren as true Christians as if the Divine grace breathed in them and imparted to them a clear knowledge of itself.

But over and above these five reasons I have a sixth that would seem to be the root from which all the others proceeded: and this is the inclination of the heavenly wheels.[2]

[1] Duarte, King of Portugal, 1433–38

[2] Azurara goes on to say that Prince Henry wanted to fulfil the predictions of his horoscope

From Azurara, G. E., *The Chronicle of the Discovery and Conquest of Guinea*, 2 vols., Hakluyt Society, 1st series, 1st vol., XCV, 1896, p.27 (**2**)

document 4

Cape Bojador

Why no ships passed this West African cape until 1434.

So the Infant, moved by these reasons, which you have already heard, began to make ready his ships and his people, as the needs of the case required; but this much you may learn, that although he sent out many times, not only ordinary men, but such as by their experience in great deeds of war were of foremost name in the profession of arms, yet there was not one who dared to pass that Cape of Bojador and learn about the land beyond it, as the Infant wished. And to say the truth this was not from cowardice or want of good will, but from the novelty of the thing and the wide-spread and ancient rumour about this Cape, that had been cherished by the mariners of Spain from generation to generation. And although this proved to be deceitful, yet since the hazarding of this attempt seemed to threaten the last evil of all, there was great doubt as to who would be the first to risk his life in such a venture. How are we, men said, to pass the bounds that our fathers set up, or what profit can result to the Infant from the perdition of our souls as well as of our bodies – for of a truth by daring any further we shall become wilful murderers of ourselves? Have there not been in Spain other princes and lords as covetous perchance of this honour as the Infant? For certainly it cannot be presumed that among so many noble men who did such great and lofty deeds for the glory of their memory, there had not been one to dare this deed. But being satisfied of the peril, and seeing no hope of honour or profit, they left off the attempt. For, said the mariners, this much is clear, that beyond this Cape there is no race of men nor place of inhabitants: nor is the land less sandy than the deserts of Libya, where there is no water, no tree, no green herb – and the sea so shallow that a whole league from land it is only a fathom deep, while the currents are so terrible that no ship having once passed the Cape, will ever be able to return.

From Azurara, G. E., *The Chronicle of the Discovery and Conquest of Guinea*, 2 vols., Hakluyt Society, 1st series, 1st vol., XCV, 1896, p.30 (**2**)

document 5

Dividing up the slaves

Azurara's awareness of the sufferings of Africans enslaved by the Portuguese.

On the next day, which was the 8th of the month of August,[1] very early in the morning, by reason of the heat, the seamen began to make ready their boats, and to take out those captives, and carry them on shore, as they were commanded. And these, placed all together in that field, were a marvellous sight; for amongst them were some white enough, fair to look upon, and well proportioned; others were less white like mulattoes; others again were as black as Ethiops, and so ugly, both in features and in body, as almost to appear (to those who saw them) the images of a lower hemisphere. But what heart could be so hard as not to be pierced with piteous feeling to see that company? For some kept their heads low and their faces bathed in tears, looking one upon another; others stood groaning very dolorously, looking up to the height of heaven, fixing their eyes upon it, crying out loudly, as if asking help of the Father of Nature; others struck their faces with the palms of their hands, throwing themselves at full length upon the ground; others made their lamentations in the manner of a dirge, after the custom of their country. And though we could not understand the words of their language, the sound of it right well accorded with the measure of their sadness. But to increase their sufferings still more, there now arrived those who had charge of the division of the captives, and who began to separate one from another, in order to make an equal partition of the fifths; and then was it needful to part fathers from sons, husbands from wives, brothers from brothers. No respect was shewn either to friends or relations, but each fell where his lot took him.

O powerful fortune, that with thy wheels doest and undoest, compassing the matters of this world as pleaseth thee, do thou at least put before the eyes of that miserable race some understanding of matters to come; that they may receive some consolation in the midst of their great sorrow. And you who are so busy in making that division of the captives, look with pity upon so much misery; and see how they cling one to the other, so that you can hardly separate them.

And who could finish that partition without very great toil? for as often as they had placed them in one part the sons, seeing their fathers in another, rose with great energy and rushed over to them; the mothers clasped their other children in their arms, and threw themselves flat on the ground with them; receiving blows with little pity for their own flesh, if only they might not be torn from them.

¹ probably 1444

From Azurara, G. E., *The Chronicle of the Discovery and Conquest of Guinea*, 2 vols., Hakluyt Society, 1st series, 1st vol., XCV, 1896, p.81
(**2**)

document 6

Cadamosto becomes an explorer

The young Venetian nobleman, Alvise da Cadamosto, joins Prince Henry's enterprise.

In the year of Our Lord 1454, I, Alvise da Ca' da Mosto, then aged about twenty-two years, found myself in our city of Venice. Having sailed to various parts of our Mediterranean Sea, I then determined to return to Flanders, where I had been once before, in the hope of profit: for my one thought was so to employ my youth by striving in every way possible to gain qualifications, that [with this experience of the world] I might [in later years] attain honourable distinction. When I had decided to go thither, as I have said, I made ready with what little money I had, and went aboard our fleet of Flanders galleys, which was under the command of Messer Marco Zen, knight. Thus, on the eighth of August of the said year, we set forth, in God's name, from Venice. Sailing southwards, and touching at the customary ports, we ultimately made the coast of Spain.

Contrary winds delayed the galleys at Capo di San Vincenzo,[1] as it is called, so that by chance I found myself at no great distance from the place where the Lord Infante Don Heurich[2] was lodged in a country estate called Reposera.[3] [Since by its remoteness from the turmoil of affairs, it was fitted for studious contemplation, he was living there very readily.] When he had news of us, he sent one of his secretaries, Antonio Conzales, to our galleys, accompanied by a Patrizio di Conti, who claimed to be a Venetian and consul of our nation in the Kingdom of Portugal – as he proved by a letter and seal from our Seignory. He was, moreover, also in the employ of the said Lord Infante. At his command they came to our galleys with samples of sugar from the Isola de Medera,[4] dragon's blood[5] and other products of his domains and islands. These he displayed in my presence to many on the galleys and asked us various questions. He said that his lord had peopled newly discovered islands hitherto uninhabited, in proof of which he cited the sugar, dragon's blood, and other good and useful wares, but that this was nothing in regard to the other and greater achievements of his lord, who had for some time past caused seas to be navigated which had never before been sailed, and had discovered the lands of many strange races, where marvels abounded. Those who had been in these parts had wrought great gain among these new peoples, turning one *soldo* into six or ten.

They related so much in this strain that I, with the others, marvelled greatly. They thus aroused in me a growing desire to go thither. I asked if the said lord permitted any who wished to sail, and was told that he did, under one of two conditions. He might fit out the caravel at his own expense and load her with merchandise; on his return he would be obliged to pay to the said lord by law and custom a quarter of all he brought back, keeping the remainder for himself: or the lord would at his own expense equip a caravel for whomsoever wished to go if he provided the cargo: then on the return, all that had been brought back from these parts would be halved. If nothing were brought back, then the charges would be at his expense. They said that it was impossible for anyone to return without great gain; if any of our nation wished to go thither, the said lord would receive them gladly and show them much favour, for he believed that in these parts they would find spices and other valuable products, and knew that the Venetians were more skilled in these affairs than any other nation.

[1] Cape St Vincent

[2] Prince Henry, then 60 years old

[3] five miles inland from Sagres

[4] Madeira

[5] a resin used for colouring

From G. R. Crone (ed.), *The Voyages of Cadamosto*, Hakluyt Society, 2nd series, LXXX, 1937, p.1 (**8**)

document 7

The Southern Cross

The first recorded mention (1455) of this constellation which could be used by navigators south of the equator to fix latitude.

CHAPTER XXXIX: THE ELEVATION OF OUR NORTH STAR; AND THE SIX STARS OPPOSITE

During the days we spent at the mouth of this river, we saw the pole star once only; it appeared very low down over the sea, therefore we could see it only when the weather was very clear. It appeared about a third of a lance above the horizon. We also had sight of six stars low down over the sea, clear, bright, and large. By the compass, they stood due south, in the following fashion.

☆ ☆ ☆ ☆ ☆
　☆

This we took to be the southern wain, though we did not see the principal star, for it would not have been possible to sight it unless we had lost the north star.

From G. R. Crone (ed.), *The Voyages of Cadamosto*, Hakluyt Society, 2nd series, LXXX, 1937, p.61 (**8**)

document 8

Fixing latitude

An early Portuguese account (c.1505).

HOW THE DEGREES OF THE SUN'S ALTITUDE ARE TO BE ADDED TO ITS DECLINATION OR THE DECLINATION TO BE DEDUCTED FROM THE ALTITUDE.

The altitude of the sun should be taken exactly at noon with the astrolabe or quadrant. He who takes it on the eleventh of March, and on the fourteenth of September, and finds it to be 90°, which is its maximum altitude, may know for certain that he is on the Equator and has it for his zenith; for at any other time except these two equinoctial days of March 11th and September 14th, the sun does not reach an altitude of 90° at the Equator. He who takes the altitude on these two days and finds it to be fifty or sixty or eighty degrees, or more or less, but still under ninety, will not have the Equator for zenith; to ascertain his latitude he must deduct the number of degrees of altitude from 90° and this will give him the number of degrees of latitude from the Equator towards either of the tropics.

Item. The astronomers have decided that the distance from the Equator towards each of the tropics should be called the torrid zone and the 'table' of the sun. The sun pursues its course in this table throughout the year; while it rises to an altitude of 90° at the Equator and the tropics, as I have said in the preceding chapter, it also ascends during the course of the twelve months in travelling between these points that number of degrees in the said torrid zone. A man may be at such a place on any of the days of the year, and when the sun rises to an altitude of 90° it will be the zenith of his table; when he finds the altitude to be 90°, let him look at the table of the sun's declinations for the declination of that day. Let him then deduct this number from the 90° and the remainder will give the degrees of latitude that he is distant from the Equator in the direction of either tropic.

From Duarte Pacheo Pereira, *Esmeraldo de situ orbis*, Hakluyt Society, 2nd series, LXXIX, 1937, p.28 (**21**)

document 9

Grant to Fernão Gomes, 1469

Gomes's contract lasted for six years.

. . . as the king [Affonso V] was very occupied with the affairs of the kingdom, and was not satisfied to cultivate this trade himself nor let it run as it was, he leased it on request in fourteen hundred and sixty-nine to Fernão Gomes, a respected citizen of Lisbon, for five years, at two hundred thousand reis a year, on condition that in each of these five years he should engage to discover one hundred leagues of coast farther on, so that at the end of the lease five hundred leagues should be discovered, beginning from Serra Leoa [Sierra Leone] . . . And among other terms of this contract was that all the ivory should be delivered to the king at the price of one thousand five hundred reis per hundredweight, . . . and – a privilege much appreciated at that time – Fernão Gomes was allowed to buy in each of the said five years one civet-cat. This contract was made in the year fourteen hundred and sixty-nine, upon condition that he was not to trade on the mainland opposite the islands of Cabo Verde, because, as they belonged to prince D. Fernando, this trade was reserved for their inhabitants. Also the traffic of Arguim was excluded, because the king had given it to his son, prince D. João, as part of his revenue; however, later on, the same Fernão Gomes secured this traffic of Arguim from the prince for some years at a price of one hundred thousand reis a year . . . And in the year fourteen hundred and seventy-four, which was the last of his lease, the king gave him a new coat of arms of nobility.

From João de Barros, *Asia*, 1552, quoted in *Europeans in West Africa*, 2 vols., Hakluyt Society, vol.I, LXXXVI, 1942, p.67 (**5**)

document 10

The building of Elmina (1481)

John II of Portugal pursued the discoveries actively, and caused the large fortress of (El)mina to be built on the Guinea coast.

As the King, D. João[1], already had in the time of his father, D. Afonso, the trade of Guiné as part of the revenue of his household, and had drawn from it gold, ivory, slaves and other things which enriched his Kingdom, and as each year new lands and peoples were discovered, his hope of the discovery of India by these seas became ever the stronger. Being a very Christian prince and lord of great prudence, he ordered the building of a fortress, to be the first stone of the Oriental Church, which he wished to build in praise and glory of God for the possession he took of that which he had discovered and which remained to be discovered, through the Pope's grant,[2] as we said before. And knowing that in the land through which ran the traffic of gold the negroes liked silk, woollen and linen clothes, and other domestic goods, that they displayed a clearer understanding than others of that coast, and that in the trade with our men they showed they would be easily converted, he commanded that this fortress should be erected in the place, where our men usually made the traffic of the gold. Thus, with the bait offered by the worldly goods which would always be obtainable there, they might receive those of the Faith through our doctrine, which was his principal aim. And though opinions in his Council about the building of this fortress were divergent because of the distance, and the ill-effects of the climate, the food of the country, and the labour of navigation upon those who went thither, the King considered that the possibility of getting even one soul to the Faith by baptism through the fortress, outweighed all the inconveniences. For he said that God would take care of them, since the work was to His praise, that his subjects would win profit, and that the patrimony of this Kingdom would be increased. Once the building of this fortress was decided upon he ordered the equipping of a Fleet of ten caravels and two *urcas*,[3] – to carry hewed stone, tiles and wood, as well as munitions and provisions for six hundred men, one hundred of whom were craftsmen and five hundred soldiers. Diogo de Azambuja, a man very experienced in the art of war, was Captain-major of these ships.

[1] John II of Portugal, 1481–95

[2] Bull of Sixtus IV, 1481

[3] large merchant ships

From João de Barros, *Asia*, 1552, quoted in *Europeans in West Africa*, 2 vols., Hakluyt Society, vol.I, LXXXVI, 1942, p.70 (**5**)

document 11

Inscription on a padroe,[1] 1482

In the absence of chronicles these padroes are important evidence for the voyages of Diogo Cão and Bartholemew Dias.

In the year 6681[2] of the creation of the world, and 1482 of the birth of our Lord Jesus, the very high, very excellent and mighty prince King João II of Portugal ordered this land to be discovered and these padroes to be placed by Diogo Cão, squire of his horses.

[1] limestone pillars brought from Portugal and erected by explorers at key points along the African coast

[2] this follows the chronology of Eusebius (*c.*260–341), generally accepted in the Middle Ages, that the world was created 5,200 years before the birth of Christ

E. Axelson, *Congo to Cape*, 1973, p.61 (**27**)

document 12

Chinese visitors?

A report made to Vasco da Gama in 1498 by inhabitants of Calicut.

It is now about 80 years since there arrived in this city of Calicut certain vessels of white Christians, who wore their hair long like Germans, and had no beards except around the mouth, such as are worn at Constantinople by cavaliers and courtiers. They landed, wearing a cuirass, helmet, and vizor, and carrying a certain weapon [sword] attached to a spear. Their vessels are armed with bombards, shorter than those in use with us. Once every two years they return with 20 or 25 vessels. They are unable to tell what people they are, nor what merchandise they bring to this city, save that it includes very fine linen-cloth and brass-ware. They load spices. Their vessels have four masts like those of Spain. If they were Germans it seems to me that we should have had some notice about them; possibly they may be Russians if they have a port there.

From E. G. Ravenstein (ed.), *First Voyage of Vasco da Gama, 1497–99*, Hakluyt Society, 1st series, XCIX, 1898, p.131 (**23**)

document 13

Arrival of Vasco da Gama, 1498

The meeting between the Portuguese and the Samorin of Calicut.

[*The King's Palace*] The further we advanced in the direction of the king's palace, the more did they increase in number. And when we arrived there, men of much distinction and great lords came out to meet the captain, and joined those who were already in attendance upon him. It was then an hour before sunset. When we reached the palace we passed through a gate into a courtyard of great size, and before we arrived at where the king was, we passed four doors, through which we had to force our way, giving many blows to the people. When, at last, we reached the door where the king was, there came forth from it a little old man, who holds a position resembling that of a bishop, and whose advice the king acts upon in all affairs of the church. This man embraced the captain when he entered the door. Several men were wounded at this door, and we only got in by the use of much force.

[*A Royal Audience, May 28*] The king was in a small court, reclining upon a couch covered with a cloth of green velvet, above which was a good mattress, and upon this again a sheet of cotton stuff, very white and fine, more so than any linen. The cushions were after the same fashion. In his left hand the king held a very large golden cup [spittoon], having a capacity of half an almude [8 pints]. At its mouth this cup was two palmas [16 inches] wide, and apparently it was massive. Into this cup the king threw the husks of a certain herb which is chewed by the people of this country because of its soothing effects, and which they call *atambor*.[1] On the right side of the king stood a basin of gold, so large that a man might just encircle it with his arms: this contained the herbs. There were likewise many silver jugs. The canopy above the couch was all gilt.

[1] betel nut

From E. G. Ravenstein (ed.), *First Voyage of Vasco da Gama, 1497–99*, Hakluyt Society, 1st series, XCIX, 1898, p.55 (**23**)

document 14

'Christians and spices'

Da Gama states his motives for coming to India.

[Arrival.] That night [May 20][1] we anchored two leagues from the city of Calecut, and we did so because our pilot mistook *Capua*, a town at that place, for Calecut. Still further there is another town called *Pandarani*. We anchored about a league and a half from the shore. After we were at anchor, four boats approached us from the land, who asked of what nation we were. We told them, and they then pointed out Calecut to us.

On the following day [May 21] these same boats came again alongside, when the captain-major sent one of the convicts to Calecut, and those with whom he went took him to two Moors from Tunis, who could speak Castilian and Genoese. The first greeting that he received was in these words: 'May the Devil take thee! What brought you hither?' They asked what he sought so far away from home, and he told them that we came in search of Christians and of spices.

[1] 1498

From E. G. Ravenstein (ed.), *First Voyage of Vasco da Gama, 1497–99*, Hakluyt Society, 1st series, XCIX, 1898 p.48 (**23**)

document 15

Presents for the king

Da Gama's gifts are inadequate.

Tuesday [May 29] the captain got ready the following things to be sent to the king, viz., twelve pieces of *lambel*, four scarlet hoods, six hats, four strings of coral, a case containing six wash-hand basins, a case of sugar, two casks of oil, and two of honey. And as it is the custom not to send anything to the king without the knowledge of the Moor, his factor, and of the *bale*, the captain informed them of his intention. They came, and when they saw the present they laughed at it, saying that it was not a thing to offer to a king, that the poorest mechant from Mecca, or any other part of India, gave more, and that if he wanted to make a present it should be in gold, as the king would not accept such things.

From E. G. Ravenstein (ed.), *First Voyage of Vasco da Gama, 1497–99*, Hakluyt Society, 1st series, XCIX, 1898, p. 60 (**23**)

document 16

Hindus of Calicut

Da Gama mistakes the Hindus for Christians.

When we arrived [at Calecut] they took us to a large church, and this is what we saw:–

The body of the church is as large as a monastery, all built of hewn stone and covered with tiles. At the main entrance rises a pillar of bronze as high as a mast, on the top of which was perched a bird, apparently a cock. In the main entrance, hung seven small bells. In this church the captain-major said his prayers, and we with him.

We did not go within the chapel, for it is the custom that only certain servants of the church, called *quafees*,[1] should enter. These *quafees* wore some threads passing over the left shoulder and under the right arm, in the same manner as our deacons wear the stole. They threw holy water over us, and gave us some white earth,[2] which the Christians of this country are in the habit of putting on their foreheads, breasts, around the neck, and on the forearms. They threw holy water upon the captain-major and gave him some of the earth, which he gave in charge of someone, giving them to understand that he would put it on later.

Many other saints were painted on the walls of the church, wearing crowns. They were painted variously, with teeth protruding an inch from the mouth, and four or five arms.

[1] these must have been Brahmin priests

[2] a mixture of ashes, cow dung, etc. used for ritual purposes

From E. G. Ravenstein (ed.), *First Voyage of Vasco da Gama, 1497–99*, Hakluyt Society, 1st series, XCIX, 1898, p. 52 (**23**)

document 17

Treatment of the Malabar sailors

An example of da Gama's ruthlessness and cruelty during his second voyage (1503). He was trying to frighten the Samorin of Calicut into submission.

Whilst they were doing this business, there came in from the offing two large ships, and twenty-two sambuks and Malabar vessels, which came from Coromandel laden with rice, which the Moors of Calecut had ordered to be laden there, as its price there was very cheap, and they gained much by it; and they came to fetch the port, thinking that our ships, if they had come, would already be at Cochym, and not at Calecut; but our fleet having sighted them, the caravels went to them, and the Moors could not fly, as they were laden, and the caravels brought them to the captain-major, and all struck their sails . . .

Then the captain-major commanded them to cut off the hands and ears and noses of all the crews, and put all that into one of the small vessels, into which he ordered them to put the friar,[1] also without ears, or nose, or hands, which he ordered to be strung round his neck, with a palm-leaf for the King, on which he told him to have a curry made to eat of what his friar brought him. When all the Indians had been thus executed, he ordered their feet to be tied together, as they had no hands with which to untie them: and in order that they should not untie them with their teeth, he ordered them to strike upon their teeth with staves, and they knocked them down their throats; and they were thus put on board, heaped up upon the top of each other, mixed up with the blood which streamed from them; and he ordered mats and dry leaves to be spread over

them, and the sails to be set for the shore, and the vessel set on fire:
and there were more than eight hundred Moors; and the small vessel
with the friar, with all the hands and ears, was also sent on shore
under sail, without being fired. These vessels went at once on shore,
where many people flocked together to put out the fire, and draw
out those whom they found alive, upon which they made great
lamentations.

[1] the 'friar' was a Hindu sent by the Samorin to sue for peace, dressed up as a friar
in order to obtain access to da Gama.

Gaspar Correa, *c*.1561, *Lendas da India*, in *The Three Voyages of Vasco
da Gama*, Hakluyt Society, 1st series, XLII, 1869, p.331 (**7**)

document 18
'The Lusiads'.

*The opening words of the most famous work in Portuguese literature,
Camoens's 'The Lusiads', which recounts the epic first voyage of Vasco da
Gama and compares his achievement to those of the heroes of classical
mythology.*

This is the story of heroes who, leaving their native Portugal behind
them, opened a way to Ceylon, and further, across seas no man had
ever sailed before. They were men of no ordinary stature, equally
at home in war and in dangers of every kind: they founded a new
kingdom among distant peoples, and made it great. It is the story
too of a line of kings who kept ever advancing the boundaries of
faith and empire, spreading havoc among the infidels of Africa and
Asia and achieving immortality through their illustrious exploits. If
my inspiration but prove equal to the task, all men shall know of
them.

  Let us hear no more then of Ulysses and Aeneas and their long
journeyings, no more of Alexander and Trajan and their famous
victories. My theme is the daring and renown of the Portuguese, to
whom Neptune and Mars alike give homage. The heroes and the
poets of old have had their day; another and loftier conception of
valour has arisen.

Luíz Vas de Camoens, *The Lusiads*, trans. William C. Atkinson,
Penguin Books, 1952, p.39 (**6**)

document 19

The Spice Islands.

Nutmeg, mace and cloves were three of the most sought-after spices. This extract is from an early sixteenth-century Portuguese source.

The Isles of Bandam

And yet further on, after leaving the Island of Timor, are five Isles near one to the other, which form as it were a roadstead in which junks are moored; which enter thereunto on both sides. These Isles they call Bandam. Both Moors and Heathen dwell therein. And in three of them grows abundance of nutmeg and mace on certain trees like unto baytrees, whereof the fruit is the nut; over it spreads the mace like a flower, and above that again another thick rind. One quintal[1] of mace is worth here as much as seven of nutmeg. The abundance is such that they burn it, and it may be had almost for the asking . . .

Maluquo

After passing these Ambam islands there are five others close to one another which they call Maluquo, wherein grow all the cloves . . . The woods of these islands are all full of certain trees like unto baytrees and their leaves are like those of the medronho [arbutus]; whereon grow the cloves in clusters.

[1] about 50 kilos

The Book of Duarte Barbosa, first published 1524, Hakluyt Society, 2nd series, XLIX, 1921, pp.196–9 (**9**)

document 20

Toscanelli's letter to Columbus, 1474.

This letter, from the Florentine humanist and cosmographer, is a key document in the history of the discoveries. It reveals one of the sources of Columbus's confidence in his own plan, and it proves that the Portuguese had already considered, and rejected, a similar scheme.

PAUL, the Physician, to Cristobal Colombo greeting. I perceive your magnificent and great desire to find a way to where the spices grow, and in reply to your letter I send you the copy of another letter which I wrote, some days ago, to a friend and favourite of the most serene King of Portugal before the wars of Castille,[1] in reply to another which, by direction of his Highness, he wrote to me on the said subject, and I send you another sea chart like the one I sent him, by which you will be satisfied respecting your enquiries: which copy is as follows:

A COPY OF THE LETTER TO MARTINS.
Paul, the Physician, to Fernan Martins, Canon at Lisbon, greeting. it was pleasant to me to understand that your health was good, and that you are in the favour and intimacy with the most generous and most magnificent Prince, your King.[2] I have already spoken with you respecting a shorter way to the places of spices than that which you take by Guinea, by means of maritime navigation. The most serene King now seeks from me some statement, or rather a demonstration to the eye, by which the slightly learned may take in and understand that way. I know this can be shown from the spherical shape of the earth, yet, to make the comprehension of it easier, and to facilitate the work, I have determined to show that way by means of a sailing chart. I, therefore, send to his Majesty a chart made by my own hands, on which are delineated your coasts and islands, whence you must begin to make your journey always westward, and the places at which you should arrive, and how far from the pole or the equinoctial line you ought to keep, and through how much space or over how many miles you should arrive at those most fertile places full of all sorts of spices and jewels. You must not be surprised if I call the parts where the spices are west, when they usually call them east, because to those always sailing west, those parts are found by navigation on the under side of the earth. But if by land and by the upper side, they will always be found to the east. The straight lines shown lengthways on the map indicate the distance from east to west, and those that are drawn across show the spaces from south to north. I have also noted on the map several places at which you may arrive for the better information of navigators, if they should reach a place different from what was expected, by reason of the wind or any other cause; and also that they may show some acquaintance with the country to the natives, which ought to be sufficiently agreeable to them. It is asserted that none but merchants live on the islands. For there the number of navigators with merchandize is so great that in all the rest of the world there are not so many as in one most noble port called Zaitun.[3] For they affirm that a hundred ships laden with pepper discharge their cargoes in that port in a single year, besides other ships bringing other spices. That country is very populous and very

rich, with a multitude of provinces and kingdoms, and with cities without number, under one prince who is called Great Kan, which name signifies *Rex Regum* in Latin, whose seat and residence is generally in the province Katay. His ancestors desired intercourse with Christians now 200 years ago. They sent to the Pope and asked for several persons learned in the faith, that they might be enlightened, but those who were sent, being impeded in their journey, went back. Also in the time of Eugenius[4] one of them came to Eugenius, who affirmed their great kindness towards Christians, and I had a long conversation with him on many subjects, about the magnitude of their rivers in length and breadth, and on the multitude of cities on the banks of the rivers. He said that on one river there were near 200 cities with marble bridges great in length and breadth, and everywhere adorned with columns. This country is worth seeking by the Latins, not only because great wealth may be obtained from it, gold and silver, all sorts of gems, and spices, which never reach us; but also on account of its learned men, philosophers, and expert astrologers, and by what skill and art so powerful and magnificent a province is governed, as well as how their wars are conducted. This is for some satisfaction to his request, so far as the shortness of time and my occupations admitted: being ready in future more fully to satisfy his royal Majesty as far as he may wish.

Given at Florence, June 24th, 1474.

LETTER TO COLUMBUS RESUMED.

From the city of Lisbon due west there are 26 spaces marked on the map, each of which has 250 miles, as far as the most noble and very great city of Quinsay.[5] For it is a hundred miles in circumference and has ten bridges, and its name signifies the city of Heaven; many wonders being related concerning it, touching the multitude of its handicrafts and resources. This space is almost a third part of the whole sphere. That city is in the province of Mangi, or near the province Katay, in which land is the royal residence. But from the island Antilia, known to you, to the most noble island of Cippangue[6] there are ten spaces. For that island is most fertile in gold, pearls, and precious stones, and they cover the temples and palaces with solid gold. Thus the spaces of sea to be crossed in the unknown parts are not great. Many things might perhaps have been declared more exactly, but a diligent thinker will be able to clear up the rest for himself. Farewell, most excellent one.

[1] Toscanelli means before the wars in the reign of Henry IV of Castile, i.e. before about 1465

² Alfonso V of Portugal, 1438–81

³ the city in Cathay described by Marco Polo

⁴ Pope Eugenius IV, 1431–47

⁵ see doc.1

⁶ Cipangu (Japan) was mentioned by Marco Polo; Antilia was a fabulous island shown on medieval maps

From C. R. Markham (ed.), *The Journal of Christopher Columbus during his First Voyage, 1492–3*, Hakluyt Society, 1st series, LXXXVI, 1893, p.3 (**17**)

document 21

Columbus's Title, 1492

The rewards promised to Columbus if he should succeed in his first voyage.

Don Ferdinand and Donna Isabella, by the grace of God King and Queen of Castile, Leon, Aragon, Sicily, Granada, Toledo, Valencia, Galicia, Majorca, Seville, Sardinia, Cordova, Corsica, Murcia, Jaen, Algarbe, Algeciras, Gibraltar, and the Canary Islands; Count and Countess of Barcelona; Lords of Biscay and Molina; Dukes of Athens and Neopatria; Counts of Roussillon and Cerdagne, Marquiscs of Oristano and Goziano; Forasmuch as you, Cristóbal Colon, are going by our command, with some of our ships and with our subjects, to discover and acquire certain islands and mainland in the ocean, and it is hoped that, by the help of God, some of the said islands and mainland in the said ocean will be discovered and acquired by your pains and industry; and as it is a just and reasonable thing that since you incur the said danger for our service you should be rewarded for it, and since we desire to honor and favor you on account of what is aforesaid, it is our will and pleasure that you, the said Cristóbal Colon, after you have discovered and acquired the said islands and mainland in the said ocean, or any of them whatsoever, shall be our Admiral of the said islands and mainland which you may thus discover and acquire, and shall be our Admiral and Viceroy and Governor therein, and shall be empowered from that time forward to call and entitle yourself Don Cristóbal Colon, and that your sons and successors in the said office and charge may likewise entitle and call themselves Don, and Admiral and Viceroy and Governor thereof; and that you may have power to use and exercise the said office of Admiral, together with the said office of Viceroy and Governor of the said islands and main-land which you may thus discover and acquire, by yourself or by your lieutenants, and to hear and determine all the suits and causes civil and criminal appertaining to the said office of Admiralty, Viceroy, and Governor according as you shall find by law, and as the Admirals of our kingdoms are accustomed to use and exercise it; and may have power to punish and chastise delinquents, and exercise the said offices of Admiralty, Viceroy, and Governor, you and your said lieutenants, in all that concerns and appertains to the said offices and to each of them; and that you shall have and levy the fees and salaries annexed, belonging and appertaining to the said offices and to each of them, according as our High Admiral in the Admiralty of our kingdoms levies and is accustomed to levy them.

From J. E. Olson and E. G. Bourne (eds.), *The Northmen, Columbus and Cabot, 985–1503*, 1906, reprinted New York, 1959, p. 81 (**19**)

document 22

Columbus's first impressions, 1492

Columbus is intrigued by the natives' friendliness, but already sees them as potential servants of the Spaniards.

[Thursday, 11 October] After sunset the Admiral returned to his original west course, and they went along at the rate of 12 miles an hour. Up to two hours after midnight they had gone 90 miles, equal 22½ leagues. As the caravel *Pinta* was a better sailer, and went ahead of the Admiral, she found the land and made the signals ordered by the Admiral. The land was first seen by a sailor named Rodrigo de Triana. But the Admiral, at ten in the previous night, being on the castle of the poop, saw a light, though it was so uncertain that he could not affirm it was land. He called Pero Gutierrez, a gentleman of the King's bedchamber, and said that there seemed to be a light, and that he should look at it. He did so, and saw it. . . . It seemed to few to be an indication of land; but the Admiral made certain that land was close. When they said the *Salve*, which all the sailors were accustomed to sing in their way, the Admiral asked and admonished the men to keep a good look-out on the forecastle, and to watch well for land; and to him who should first cry out that he saw land, he would give a silk doublet, besides the other rewards promised by the Sovereigns, which were 10,000 maravedis to him who should first see it. At two hours after midnight the land was sighted at a distance of two leagues. . . . The vessels were hove to, waiting, for day-light; and on Friday they arrived at a small island of the Lucayos, called, in the language of the Indians, *Guanahani*.[1] Presently they saw naked people. The Admiral went on shore in the armed boat, and Martin Alonso Pinzon, and Vicente Yañez, his brother, who was captain of the *Niña*. The Admiral took the royal standard, and the captains went with two banners of the green cross, which the Admiral took in all the ships as a sign. . . .

Presently many inhabitants of the island assembled. What follows is in the actual words of the Admiral in his book of the first navigation and discovery of the Indies. 'I,' he says, 'that we might form a great friendship, for I knew that they were a people who could more easily be freed and converted to our holy faith by love than by force, gave to some of them red caps, and glass beads to put round their necks, and many other things of little value, which gave them great pleasure, and made them so much our friends that it was a marvel to see. They afterwards came to the ship's boats where we were, swimming and bringing us parrots, cotton threads in skeins, darts and many other things; and we exchanged them for other things that we gave them, such as glass beads and small bells. In fine, they took all, and gave what they had with good will. It appeared to me to be a race of people very poor in everything. They go as naked as when their mothers bore them, and so do the women, although I did not see more than one young girl. All I saw were youths, none more than thirty years of age. They are very well made, with very handsome bodies, and very good countenances. Their hair is short and coarse, almost like the hair of a horse's tail. They wear the hair brought down to the eye-brows, except a few locks behind, which they wear long and never cut. They paint themselves black, and they are the colour of the Canarians, neither black nor white. . . . They neither carry nor know anything of arms; for I showed them swords, and they took them by the blade and cut themselves through ignorance. They have no iron, their darts being wands without iron, some of them having a fish's tooth at the end, and others being pointed in various ways. . . . I saw some with marks of wounds on their bodies, and I made signs to ask what it was, and they gave me to understand that people from other adjacent islands came with the intention of seizing them, and that they defended themselves. I believed, and still believe, that they come here from the mainland to take them prisoners. They should be good servants and intelligent, and I observed that they quickly took in what was said to them, and I believe that they would easily be made Christians, as it appeared to me that they had no religion, I, our Lord being pleased, will take hence, at the time of my departure, six natives for your Highnesses, that they may learn to speak. I saw no beast of any kind except parrots, on this island.'

[1] Watling's Island, alias San Salvador, in the Bahamas

From *The Journal of Christopher Columbus*, trans. C. Jane, revised L. A. Vigneras, 1960, p. 36; quoted in J. H. Parry (ed.), *The European Reconnaissance*, 1968, p. 154 (**20**)

document 23

Loss of the Santa Maria

Another extract from Columbus's Journal.

TUESDAY, 25TH OF DECEMBER. CHRISTMAS.
Navigating yesterday, with little wind, from *Santo Tomé* to *Punta Santa*[1] and being a league from it, at about eleven o'clock at night the Admiral went down to get some sleep, for he had not had any rest for two days and a night. As it was calm, the sailor who steered the ship thought he would go to sleep, leaving the tiller in charge of a boy. The Admiral had forbidden this throughout the voyage, whether it was blowing or whether it was calm. The boys were never to be entrusted with the helm. The Admiral had no anxiety respecting sand-banks and rocks, because, when he sent the boats to that king on Sunday, they had passed to the east of *Punta Santa* at least three leagues and a half, and the sailors had seen all the coast, and the rocks there are from *Punta Santa*, for a distance of three leagues to the E.S.E. They saw the course that should be taken, which had not been the case before, during this voyage. It pleased our Lord that, at twelve o'clock at night, when the Admiral had retired to rest, and when all had fallen asleep, seeing that it was a dead calm and the sea like glass, the tiller being in the hands of a boy, the current carried the ship on one of the sand-banks. If it had not been night the bank could have been seen, and the surf on it could be heard for a good league. But the ship ran upon it so gently that it could scarcely be felt. The boy, who felt the helm and heard the rush of the sea, cried out. The Admiral at once came up,

and so quickly that no one had felt that the ship was aground. Presently the master of the ship,[2] whose watch it was, came on deck. The Admiral ordered him and others to launch the boat, which was on the poop, and lay out an anchor astern. The master, with several others, got into the boat, and the Admiral thought that they did so with the object of obeying his orders. But they did so in order to take refuge with the caravel, which was half a league to leeward. The caravel would not allow them to come on board, acting judiciously, and they therefore returned to the ship; but the caravel's boat arrived first. When the Admiral saw that his own people fled in this way, the water rising and the ship being across the sea, seeing no other course, he ordered the masts to be cut away and the ship to be lightened as much as possible, to see if she would come off. But, as the water continued to rise, nothing more could be done. Her side fell over across the sea, but it was nearly calm. Then the timbers opened, and the ship was lost.

[1] points on the north coast of Hispaniola

[2] Juan de la Cosa, later a cartographer and explorer in his own right

From C. R. Markham, (ed.) *The Journal of Christopher Columbus during his First Voyage, 1492–3*, Hakluyt Society. 1st series, LXXXVI, 1893 p. 3 (**17**)

document 24

Treaty of Tordesillas, 1494

The famous line of demarcation which, although in practice impossible to calculate accurately, allowed Spain and Portugal to continue to pursue their respective explorations without coming to blows.

Thereupon it was declared by the above-mentioned representatives of the aforesaid King and Queen of Castile, Leon, Aragon, Sicily, Granada, etc, and of the aforesaid King of Portugal and the Algarves, etc[1]:

[1.] That, whereas a certain controversy exists between the said lords, their constituents, as to what lands, of all those discovered in the ocean sea up to the present day, the date of this treaty, pertain to each one of the said parts respectively; therefore, for the sake of peace and concord, and for the preservation of the relationship and love of the said King of Portugal for the said King and Queen of Castile, Aragon, etc., it being the pleasure of their Highnesses, they, their said representatives, acting in their name and by virtue of their powers herein described, covenanted and agreed that a boundary or straight line be determined and drawn north and south, from pole to pole, on the said ocean sea, from the Arctic to the Antarctic pole. This boundary or line shall be drawn straight, as aforesaid, at a distance of three hundred and seventy leagues[2] west of the Cape Verde Islands, being calculated by degrees, or by any other manner as may be considered the best and readiest, provided the distance shall be no greater than abovesaid. And all lands, both islands and mainlands, found and discovered already, or to be found and discovered hereafter, by the said King of Portugal and by his vessels on this side of the said line and bound determined as above, toward the east, in either north or south latitude, on the eastern side of the said bound, provided the said bound is not crossed, shall belong to, and remain in the possession of, and pertain forever to, the said King of Portugal and his successors. And all other lands, both islands and mainlands, found or to be found hereafter, discovered or to be discovered hereafter, which have been discovered or shall be discovered by the said King and Queen of Castile, Aragon, etc., and by their vessels, on the western side of the said bound, determined as above, after having passed the said bound toward the west, in either its north or south latitude, shall belong to, and remain in the possession of, and pertain forever to, the said King and Queen of Castile, Leon, etc., and to their successors.

[1] Ferdinand and Isabella, and John II

[2] a league was just over three modern nautical miles

European Treaties bearing upon the History of the United States, 4 vols., Washington, 1917–37, 1st vol., ed. F. G. Davenport, 1917, p. 95 (**10**)

document 25
Vespucci's appointment as Chief Pilot of Spain, 1505

Amerigo Vespucci was the first to hold the important office of Pilot Major to the Casa de Contratación *in Seville. He held the post until his death in 1512.*

Seeing that it has come to our[1] notice, and that we have seen by experience, that, owing to the pilots not being so expert as is necessary, nor so well instructed in what they ought to know, so as to be competent to rule and govern the ships that navigate in the voyage over the Ocean Sea to our islands and mainland which we possess in the Indies; and that through their default, either in not knowing how to rule and govern, or through not knowing how to find the altitude by the quadrant or astrolabe, nor the methods of calculating it, have happened many disasters, and those who have sailed under their governance have been exposed to great danger, by which our Lord has been ill-served, as well as our finances, while the merchants who trade thither have received much hurt and loss. And for a remedy to the above, and because it is necessary, as well for that navigation as for other voyages by which, with the help of our Lord, we hope to make new discoveries in other lands, that there should be persons who are more expert and better instructed, and who know the things necessary for such navigation, so that those who are under them may go more safely, it is our will and pleasure, and we order that all the pilots of our kingdoms and lordships, who are now or shall hereafter be appointed as pilots in the said navigation to the islands and mainland that we possess in the parts of the Indies, and in other parts of the Ocean Sea, shall be instructed and shall know what it is necessary for them to know respecting the quadrant and astrolabe, in order that, by uniting theory with practice, they may be able to make good use of them in the said voyages made to the said parts, and, without such knowledge, no one shall go in the said ships as pilots, nor receive pay as pilots, nor may the masters receive them on board ship, until they have first been examined by you, Amerigo Despuchi, our Chief Pilot, and they shall be given by you a certificate of examination and approval touching the knowledge of each one. Holding the said certificates, we order that they shall be taken and received as expert pilots by whoever is shown them, for it is our pleasure that you shall be examiner of the said pilots.

[1] Ferdinand of Aragon

From C. R. Markham, (ed.) *The Letters of Amerigo Vespucci*, Hakluyt Society, 1st series, XC, 1894, p. 63 (**24**)

document 26

Vespucci and the New World

Part of a letter written by Amerigo Vespucci describing his voyage of 1501 along the coasts of Brazil and Patagonia. It was after reports of this voyage that Waldseemüller made the suggestion that Vespucci's name should be given to the new continent.

MARCH (OR APRIL) 1503.

Alberico Vesputio to Lorenzo Pietro di Medici, salutation. In passed days I wrote very fully to you of my return from the new countries, which have been found and explored with the ships, at the cost, and by the command, of this Most Serene King of Portugal; and it is lawful to call it a new world, because none of these countries were known to our ancestors, and to all who hear about them they will be entirely new. For the opinion of the ancients was, that the greater part of the world beyond the equinoctial line to the south was not land, but only sea, which they have called the Atlantic; and if they have affirmed that any continent is there, they have given many reasons for denying that it is inhabited. But this their opinion is false, and entirely opposed to the truth. My last voyage has proved it, for I have found a continent in that southern part; more populous and more full of animals than our Europe, or Asia, or Africa, and even more temperate and pleasant than any other region known to us, as will be explained further on.

From C. R. Markham, (ed.) *The Letters of Amerigo Vespucci*, Hakluyt Society, 1st series, XC, 1894, p. 42 (**24**)

document 27

The battle with the Tlaxcalans

Before reaching Tenochtitlan, the capital of the Aztec empire, Cortés had to cross the territory of the Tlaxcalans, who launched repeated attacks against the Spaniards. Only after their defeat did this tribe become Cortés's staunchest ally.

Thus all the plain was swarming with warriors and we stood four hundred men in number, and of those many sick and wounded. And we knew for certain that this time our foe came with the determination to leave none of us alive excepting those who would be sacrificed to their idols.

To go back to our battle: How they began to charge on us! What a hail of stones sped from their slings! As for their bowmen, the javelins lay like corn on the threshing floor; all of them barbed and fire-hardened, which would pierce any armour and would reach the vitals where there is no protection; the men with swords and shields and other arms larger than swords, such as broadswords, and lances, how they pressed on us and with what valour and what mighty shouts and yells they charged upon us! The steady bearing of our artillery, musketeers and crossbowmen, was indeed a help to us, and we did the enemy much damage, and those of them who came close to us with their swords and broadswords met with such sword play from us that they were forced back and they did not close in on us so often as in the last battle. The horsemen were so skilful and bore themselves so valiantly that, after God who protected us, they were our bulwark. However, I saw that our troops were in considerable confusion, so that neither the shouts of Cortés nor the other captains availed to make them close up their ranks, and so many Indians charged down on us that it was only by a miracle of sword play that we could make them give way so that our ranks could be reformed. One thing only saved our lives, and that was that the enemy were so numerous and so crowded one on another that the shots wrought havoc among them, and in addition to this they were not well commanded, for all the captains with their forces could not come into action, and from what we knew, since the last battle had been fought, there had been disputes and quarrels between the Captain Xicotenga and another captain the son of Chichimecateclc, over what the one had said to the other, that he had not fought well in the previous battle; to this the son of Chichimecateclc replied that he had fought better [than Xicotenga] and was ready to prove it by personal combat. So in this battle Chichimecateclc and his men would not help Xicotenga, and we knew for a certainty that he had also called on the company of Huexotzinco to abstain from fighting. Besides this, ever since the last battle they were afraid of the horses and the musketry, and the swords and crossbows, and our hard fighting; above all was the mercy of God which gave us strength to endure. So Xicotenga was not obeyed by two of the commanders, and we were doing great damage to his men, for we were killing many of them, and this they tried to conceal; for as they were so numerous, whenever one of their men was wounded, they immediately bound him up and carried him off on their shoulders, so that in this battle, as in the last, we never saw a dead man.

The enemy were already losing heart, and knowing that the followers of the other two captains whom I have already named, would not come to their assistance, they began to give way. It seems that in that battle we had killed one very important captain, not to mention others, and the enemy began to retreat in good order, our horsemen following them at a hand gallop for a short distance, for they could not sit their horses for fatigue, and when we found ourselves free from that multitude of warriors, we gave thanks to God.

From Bernal Díaz del Castillo, *The True History of the Conquest of New Spain*, 5 vols., Hakluyt Society, 2nd series, (ed.) A. P. Maudslay, vol. I, XXIII, 1908, p. 238 (**11**)

document 28

Montezuma, emperor of the Aztecs

Montezuma's power was more absolute than that of any European monarch.

OF THE MANNER AND APPEARANCE OF THE GREAT MONTEZUMA
AND WHAT A GREAT PRINCE HE WAS.

The great Montezuma was about forty years old, of good height and well proportioned, slender, and spare of flesh, not very swarthy, but of the natural colour and shade of an Indian. He did not wear his hair long, but so as just to cover his ears, his scanty black beard was well shaped and thin. His face was somewhat long, but cheerful, and he had good eyes and showed in his appearance and manner both tenderness and, when necessary, gravity. He was very neat and clean and bathed once every day in the afternoon. He had many women as mistresses, daughters of Chieftains, and he had two great Cacicas[1] as his legitimate wives, and when he had intercourse with them it was so secretly that no one knew anything about it, except some of his servants. He was free from unnatural offences. The clothes that he wore one day, he did not put on again until four days later. He had over two hundred chieftains in his guard, in other rooms close to his own, not that all were meant to converse with him, but only one or another, and when they went to speak to him they were obliged to take off their rich mantles and put on others of little worth, but they had to be clean, and they had to enter barefoot with their eyes lowered to the ground, and not to look up in his face. And they made him three obeisances, and said: 'Lord, my Lord, my Great Lord,' before they came up to him, and then they made their report and with a few words he dismissed them, and on taking leave they did not turn their backs, but kept their faces toward him with their eyes to the ground, and they did not turn their backs until they left the room. I noticed another thing, that when other great chiefs came from distant lands about disputes or

business, when they reached the apartments of the Great Monte
zuma, they had to come barefoot and with poor mantles, and they
might not enter directly into the Palace, but had to loiter about a
little on one side of the Palace door, for to enter hurriedly was
considered to be disrespectful.

[1] the daughters of Caciques (chiefs)

From Bernal Díaz del Castillo, *The True History of the Conquest of New
Spain*, 5 vols., Hakluyt Society, 2nd series, trans. A. P. Maudslay,
vol. 2, XXIV, 1910, p. 60 (**11**)

document 29

The marketplace at Tenochtitlan

*On entering the Aztec capital the Spaniards were overwhelmed by its size and
prosperity, so much greater than any Spanish city.*

When we arrived at the great market place, called Tlaltelolco, we
were astounded at the number of people and the quantity of
merchandise that it contained, and at the good order and control
that was maintained, for we had never seen such a thing before. The
chieftains who accompanied us acted as guides. Each kind of
merchandise was kept by itself and had its fixed place marked out.
Let us begin with the dealers in gold, silver, and precious stones,
feathers, mantles, and embroidered goods. Then there were other
wares consisting of Indian slaves both men and women: and I say
that they bring as many of them to that great market for sale as the
Portuguese bring negroes from Guinea; and they brought them
along tied to long poles, with collars round their necks so that they
could not escape, and others they left free. Next there were other
traders who sold great pieces of cloth and cotton, and articles of
twisted thread, and there were *cacahuateros* who sold cacao. In this
way one could see every sort of merchandise that is to be found in
the whole of New Spain, placed in arrangement in the same manner
as they do in my own country, which is Medina del Campo, where
they hold the fairs, where each line of booths has its particular kind
of merchandise, and so it is in this great market. There were those
who sold cloths of hencquen and ropes and the *cotaras*[1] with which
they are shod, which are made from the same plant, and sweet
cooked roots, and other tubers which they get from this plant, all
were kept in one part of the market in the place assigned to them.

In another part there were skins of tigers and lions, of otters and jackals, deer and other animals and badgers and mountain cats, some tanned and others untanned, and other classes of merchandise.

Let us go on and speak of these who sold beans and sage and other vegetables and herbs in another part, and to those who sold fowls, cocks with wattles, rabbits, hares, deer, mallards, young dogs and other things of that sort in their part of the market, and let us also mention the fruiterers, and the women who sold cooked food, dough and tripe in their own part of the market; then every sort of pottery made in a thousand different forms from great water jars to little jugs, these also had a place to themselves; then those who sold honey and honey paste and other dainties like nut paste, and those who sold lumber, boards, cradles, beams, blocks and benches, each article by itself, and the vendors of *ocote*[2] firewood, and other things of a similar nature. I must furthermore mention, asking your pardon, that they also sold many canoes full of human excrement, and these were kept in the creeks near the market, and this they use to make salt or for tanning skins, for without it they say that they cannot be well prepared. I know well that some gentlemen laugh at this, but I say that it is so, and I may add that on all the roads it is a usual thing to have places made of reeds or straw or grass, so that they may be screened from the passers by, into these they retire when they wish to purge their bowels so that even that filth should not be lost. But why do I waste so many words in recounting what they sell in that great market, for I shall never finish if I tell it all in detail. Paper, which in this country is called *Amal*, and reeds scented with *liquidambar*, and full of tobacco, and yellow ointments and things of that sort are sold by themselves, and much cochineal is sold under the arcades which are in that great market place, and there are many vendors of herbs and other sorts of trades. There are also buildings where three magistrates sit in judgement, and there are executive officers like *Alguacils* who inspect the merchandise. I am forgetting those who sell salt, and those who make the stone knives, and how they split them off the stone itself; and the fisherwomen and others who sell some small cakes made fom a sort of ooze which they get out of the great lake, which curdles, and from this they make a bread having a flavour something like cheese. There are for sale axes of brass and copper and tin, and gourds and gaily painted jars made of wood. I could wish that I had finished telling of all the things which are sold there, but they are so numerous and of such different quality and the great market place with its surrounding arcades was so crowded with people, that one would not have been able to see and inquire about it all in two days.

¹ sandals

² pitchpine

From Bernal Díaz del Castillo, *The True History of the Conquest of New Spain*, trans. A. P. Maudslay, Hakluyt Society, 1st series, 5 vols., vol. 2, XXIV, 1910, p. 70 (**11**)

document 30
The state of the capital after the defeat of the Aztecs

The aftermath of the final campaign by Cortés.

Let us leave this and let us speak of the dead bodies and heads that were in the houses where Guatemoc had taken refuge. I say on my oath, Amen, that all the houses and the palisades in the lake were full of heads and corpses and I do not know how to describe it for in the streets and courts of Tlatelolco there was no difference, and we could not walk except among corpses and heads of dead Indians. I have read about the destruction of Jerusalem but I know not for certain if there was greater mortality than this, for of the great number of the warriors from all the provinces and towns subject to Mexico who had crowded in [to the city] most of them died, and as I have already said, thus the land and the lake and the palisades were all full of dead bodies, and stank so much that no one could endure it, and for this reason, as soon as Guatemoc was captured, each one of the Captains went to his own camp, as I have already said, and even Cortés was ill from the stench which assailed his nostrils, and from headache, during the days we were in Tlatelolco. . . .

Let us stop speaking of this until later on, and say that as there was so great a stench in the city, Guatemoc asked permission of Cortés for all the Mexican forces left in the city to go out to the neighbouring pueblos, and they were promptly told to do so. I assert that during three days and nights they never ceased streaming out and all three causeways were crowded with men, women and children, so thin, yellow, dirty and stinking, that it was pitful to see them. When the city was free of them, Cortés went to examine it and we found the houses full of corpses and there were some poor Mexicans, who could not move out, still among them, and what they excreted from their bodies was a filth such as thin swine pass which have been fed upon nothing but grass, and all the city was as though it had been ploughed up and the roots of the herbs dug out and they had eaten them and even cooked the bark of some of the trees, and there was no fresh water to be found, only salt water. I also wish to state that they did not eat the flesh of their own Mexicans, only that of our people and our Tlaxcalan allies whom they had captured, and there had been no births for a long time, as they had suffered so much from hunger and thirst and continual fighting.

From Bernal Díaz del Castillo, *The True History of the Conquest of New Spain*, trans A. P. Maudslay, Hakluyt Society, 1st series, 5 vols., vol. 4, XXX, 1912, p. 185 (**11**)

document 31

Balboa discovers the Pacific, 1513

The Isthmus of Panama, which Balboa had crossed, runs from east to west, so he christened his new ocean the South Sea, a name which the Spanish retained for some time.

And on the twenty-ninth of the month, St Michael's Day, Vasco Núñez[1] named twenty-six men, those who seemed to him best fitted, to accompany him with their arms, and left the rest of his force encamped at the village of Chape[2]. He marched with this party down to the shore of the South Sea, to the bay which they had named Saint Michael, which was about half a league from their camp. They found a large inlet, lined with forest, and emerged on to the beach about the hour of vespers. The water was low, and great areas of mud exposed; so they sat by the shore waiting for the tide to rise, which presently it did, rushing into the bay with great speed and force. Then Captain Vasco Núñez held up a banner with a picture of the Blessed Virgin, Our Lady, with her precious Son Our Lord Jesus Christ in her arms, and below, the royal arms of Castile and León; and with his drawn sword in his hand and his shield on his arm, he waded into the salt sea up to his knees, and paced back and forth, reciting 'Long live the most high and most mighty monarchs, Don Fernando and Doña Juana, sovereigns of Castile and Aragon and Navarre, etc., in whose names, and for the royal crown of Castile, I now take possession, in fact and in law, of these southern seas, lands, coasts, harbors and islands, with all territories, kingdoms and provinces which belong to them or may be acquired, in whatever manner, for whatever reason, by whatever title, ancient or modern, past, present or future, without let or hindrance. And if any other prince, Christian or infidel, of whatever allegiance, standing or belief, should claim any right to these lands or seas, I am ready and armed to defy him and defend them in the name of the Kings of Castile, present and future, who hold authority and dominion over these Indies, both islands and mainland, from Arctic to Antarctic, on both sides of the Equinoctial Line, within and without the Tropics of Cancer and of Capricorn, as most fully, completely and lawfully belongs to Their Majesties, their heirs and successors for ever,

[1] Balboa

[2] on the isthmus of Panama

From Gonzalo Fernandez de Oviedo, *General and Natural History of the Indies*, 1535, trans. J. H. Parry in *The European Reconnaissance, Selected Documents*, 1968, p. 234 (**20**)

document 32

Pizarro ambushes Atahualpa

In this one decisive action Pizarro encompassed the defeat of the Inca empire.

Very soon they saw the plain full of men, halting at intervals, to wait for those who were filing out of the camp. The march of the troops along the road continued until the afternoon; and they came in separate detachments. Having passed all the narrow places on the road, they reached the ground close to the camp of the Christians, and still troops kept issuing from the camp of the Indians. Presently the Governor ordered all the Spaniards to arm themselves secretly in their lodgings, and to keep the horses saddled and bridled, and under the orders of three captains, but none were to show themselves in the open space. The Captain of the artillery was ordered to have his guns pointed towards the enemy on the plain, and, when the time came, to fire. Men were stationed in the streets leading to the open space, and, taking twenty men with him, the Governor went to his lodging. These had the duty entrusted to them of seizing the person of Atabaliba, if he should come cautiously with so large a force as was coming; but the Governor ordered that he should be taken alive. All the troops had orders not to leave their quarters, even if the enemy should enter the open space, until they should hear the guns fired off. The sentries were to be on the alert, and, if they saw that the enemy intended treachery, they were to give the signal; and all were to sally out of the lodgings, the cavalry mounted, when they heard the cry of *Santiago*.

Having made these arrangements, the Governor waited for the appearance of Atabaliba; but no Christian was in sight except the sentry, who gave notice of what was passing in the army of the Indians. The Governor and Captain-General visited the quarters of the Spaniards, seeing that they were ready to sally forth when it was necessary, saying to them all that they must be of good courage, and make fortresses of their hearts, for that they had no others, and no hope but in God, who would help those who worked in his service, even in their greatest need. He told them that though, for every Christian, there were five hundred Indians, yet they must have that reliance which good men find on such occasions, and they must trust that God would fight on their side. He told them that, at the moment of attacking, they must come out with desperate fury and break through the enemy, taking care that the horses do not hinder each other. These and similar exhortations were made by the Governor and Captain-General to the Christians, to raise their spirits, and they were more ready to come forth than to remain in their lodgings. Each man was ready to encounter a hundred, and they felt very little fear at seeing so great a multitude.

When the Governor saw that it was near sunset, and that Atabaliba did not move from the place to which he had repaired, although troops still kept issuing out of his camp, he sent a Spaniard to ask him to come into the square to see him before it was dark. As soon as the messenger came before Atabaliba, he made an obeisance to him, and made signs that he should come to where the Governor waited. Presently he and his troops began to move, and the Spaniard returned and reported that they were coming, and that the men in front carried arms concealed under their clothes, which were strong tunics of cotton, beneath which were stones and bags and slings; all which made it appear that they had a treacherous design. Soon the van of the enemy began to enter the open space. First came a squadron of Indians dressed in a livery of different colours, like a chess board. They advanced, removing the straws from the ground, and sweeping the road. Next came three squadrons in different dresses, dancing and singing. Then came a number of men with armour, large metal plates, and crowns of gold and silver. Among them was Atabaliba in a litter lined with plumes of macaws' feathers, of many colours, and adorned with plates of gold and

silver. Many Indians carried it on their shoulders on high. Next
came two other litters and two hammocks, in which were some principal chiefs; and lastly, several squadrons of Indians with crowns
of gold and silver.

As soon as the first entered the open space they moved aside and
gave space to the others. On reaching the centre of the open space,
Atabaliba remained in his litter on high, and the others with him,
while his troops did not cease to enter. A captain then came to the
front and, ascending the fortress near the open space, where the
artillery was posted, raised his lance twice, as for a signal. Seeing
this, the Governor asked the Father Friar Vicente if he wished to
go and speak to Atabaliba, with an interpreter? He replied that he
did wish it, and he advanced, with a cross in one hand and the Bible
in the other, and going amongst the troops up to the place where
Atabaliba was, thus addressed him: 'I am a Priest of God, and I
teach Christians the things of God, and in like manner I come to
teach you. What I teach is that which God says to us in this Book.
Therefore, on the part of God and of the Christians, I beseech you
to be their friend, for such is God's will, and it will be for your good.
Go and speak to the Governor, who waits for you.'

Atabaliba asked for the Book, that he might look at it, and the
Priest gave it to him closed. Atabaliba did not know how to open
it, and the Priest was extending his arm to do so, when Atabaliba,
in great anger, gave him a blow on the arm, not wishing that it
should be opened. Then he opened it himself, and, without any
astonishment at the letters and paper, as had been shown by other
Indians, he threw it away from him five or six paces, and, to the
words which the monk had spoken to him through the interpreter,
he answered with much scorn, saying: 'I know well how you have
behaved on the road, how you have treated my Chiefs, and taken
the cloth from my storehouses.' The Monk replied: 'The Christians
have not done this, but some Indians took the cloth without the
knowledge of the Governor, and he ordered it to be restored.'
Atabaliba said: 'I will not leave this place until they bring it all to me.'
The Monk returned with this reply to the Governor. Atabaliba
stood up on the top of the litter, addressing his troops and ordering
them to be prepared. The Monk told the Governor what had passed
between him and Atabaliba, and that he had thrown the Scriptures
to the ground. Then the Governor put on a jacket of cotton, took
his sword and dagger, and with the Spaniards who were with him,
entered amongst the Indians most valiantly; and with only four men
who were able to follow him, he came to the litter where Atabaliba

115

was, and fearlessly seized him by the arm, crying out *Santiago*. Then the guns were fired off, the trumpets were sounded, and the troops, both horse and foot, sallied forth. On seeing the horses charge, many of the Indians who were in the open space fled, and such was the force with which they ran that they broke down part of the wall surrounding it, and many fell over each other. The horsemen rode them down, killing and wounding, and following in pursuit. The infantry made so good an assault upon those that remained that in a short time most of them were put to the sword. The Governor still held Atabaliba by the arm, not being able to pull him out of the litter because he was raised so high. Then the Spaniards made such a slaughter amongst those who carried the litter that they fell to the ground, and, if the Governor had not protected Atabaliba, that proud man would there have paid for all the cruelties he had committed. The Governor, in protecting Atabaliba, received a slight wound in the hand. During the whole time no Indian raised his arms against a Spaniard. So great was the terror of the Indians at seeing the Governor force his way through them, at hearing the fire of the artillery, and beholding the charging of the horses, a thing never before heard of, that they thought more of flying to save their lives than of fighting. All those who bore the litter of Atabaliba appeared to be principal chiefs. They were all killed, as well as those who were carried in the other litters and hammocks.

Report of Francisco de Xeres, secretary to Francisco Pizarro, in C. R. Markham (ed), *Reports on the Discovery of Peru*, Hakluyt Society, 1st series, XLVII, 1972, p. 51 (**26**)

document 33

Atahualpa's ransom

The Incas kept their side of this bargain but the Spaniards did not, and Atahualpa was executed shortly after the gold and silver had been collected.

Atabaliba feared that the Spaniards would kill him, so he told the Governor, that he would give his captors a great quantity of gold and silver. The Governor asked him: 'How much can you give, and in what time?' Atabaliba said: 'I will give gold enough to fill a room twenty-two feet long and seventeen wide, up to a white line which is half way up the wall.' The height would be that of a man's stature and a half. He said that, up to that mark, he would fill the room with different kinds of golden vessels, such as jars, pots, vases, besides lumps and other pieces. As for silver, he said he would fill the whole chamber with it twice over. He undertook to do this in two months. The Governor told him to send off messengers with this object, and that, when it was accomplished, he need have no fear. Then Atabaliba sent messages to his captains, who were in the city of Cuzco, ordering them to send two thousand Indians laden with gold and silver, without counting that which was coming with his brother, whom they were bringing as a prisoner.

Report of Francisco de Xeres, secretary to Francisco Pizarro, in C. R. Markham (ed.), *Reports on the Discovery of Peru*, Hakluyt Society, 1st series, XLVII, 1972, p. 61 (**26**)

document 34

Magellan's project

Magellan hoped to find a way through, or round, the newly discovered coastlines of America.

And though there was a certain rumour afloat that the Portuguese had progressed so far to the east as to cross their own limits and enter the territory of the Spaniards, and that Malacca and the Great Bay were within our limits, still all these things were said rather than believed, until four years ago Ferdinand Magellan, a distinguished Portuguese, who, for many years had explored the coasts of the whole of the East as Admiral, took a great hatred to his king, whom he complained of as being most ungrateful to him, and showed Cæsar[1] that though it was not yet quite sure whether Malacca was within the confines of the Spaniards or the Portuguese, because, as yet, nothing of the longitude had been clearly proved, yet that it was quite plain that the Great Gulf and the people of Sinae[2] lay within the Spanish boundary. This, too, was held to be most certain, that the islands which they call the Moluccas, in which all the spices are produced, and are thence exported to Malacca, lay within the Spanish western division, and that it was possible to sail there; and that spices could be brought thence to Spain more easily, and at less expense and cheaper, as they came direct from their native place.

Their course would be this, to sail westward, coasting the southern hemisphere (till they came) to the East. The thing seemed almost impossible and useless, not because it was thought a difficult thing to go from the west right to the east under the hemisphere, but because it was uncertain whether ingenious nature, which has done nothing without the greatest foresight, had not so dissevered the east from the west, partly by sea and partly by land, as to make it impossible to arrive there by either land or sea travelling. For it had not then been discovered whether that great region which is called Terra Firma did separate the western sea from the eastern; it was clear enough that that continent, in its southern part, trended southwards and afterwards westwards. It was clear, also, that two regions had been discovered in the North, one of which they called Regio Bacalearum (Cod-fish Land), from a new kind of fish; and the other Terra Florida. And if these two were united to that Terra Firma, it was impossible to get to the east by going from the west, as nothing had ever been discovered of any channel through this land, though it had been sought for most diligently and with great labour. And they considered it a very doubtful and most dangerous enterprise to go through the limits of the Portuguese, and so to the east. For which reason it seemed to Cæsar and to his counsellors that these men were promising a thing from which much was to be hoped, but still of great difficulty.

[1] Charles V

[2] terms taken from Ptolemy's *Geography*

From a letter from Maximilianus Transylvanus to the Most Reverend Cardinal of Salzburg, in *Magellan's First Voyage round the World*, trans. Lord Stanley of Alderney, Hakluyt Society, 1st series, LII, 1874, p. 186 (**22**)

Patagonian giants

document 35

The myth started here by Pigafetta, Magellan's companion and chronicler, that Patagonia was peopled by giants persisted until the eighteenth century.

Departing thence as far as forty nine degrees and a half in the Antarctic heavens[1] (as we were in the winter), we entered into a port to pass the winter, and remained there two whole months without ever seeing anybody. However, one day, without anyone expecting it, we saw a giant, who was on the shore of the sea, quite naked, and was dancing and leaping, and singing, and whilst singing he put the sand and dust on his head. Our captain sent one of his men towards him, whom he charged to sing and leap like the other to reassure him, and show him friendship. This he did, and immediately the sailor led this giant to a little island where the captain was waiting for him: and when he was before us he began to be astonished, and to be afraid, and he raised one finger on high, thinking that we came from heaven. He was so tall that the tallest of us only came up to his waist; however he was well built. He had a large face, painted red all round, and his eyes also were painted yellow around them, and he had two hearts painted on his cheeks; he had but little hair on his head, and it was painted white. When he was brought before the captain he was clothed with the skin of a certain beast, which skin was very skilfully sewed. This beast[2] has its head and ears of the size of a mule, and the neck and body of the fashion of a camel, the legs of a deer, and the tail like that of a horse, and it neighs like a horse. There is a great quantity of these animals in this same place. This giant had his feet covered with the skin of this animal in the form of shoes, and he carried in his hand a short and thick bow, with a thick cord made of the gut of the said beast, with a bundle of cane arrows, which were not very long, and were feathered like ours, but they had no iron at the end, though they had at the end some small white and black cut stones, and those arrows were like those which the Turks use. The captain caused food and drink to be given to this giant, then they showed him some things, amongst others, a steel mirror. When the giant saw his likeness in it, he was greatly terrified, leaping backwards, and made three or four of our men fall down.

[1] 49½ degrees south, i.e. well down the Patagonian coast

[2] the guanaca, a kind of llama

From Antonio Pigafetta, *Magellan's First Voyage round the World*, trans. Lord Stanley of Alderney, Hakluyt Society, 1st series, LII, 1874, p. 49 (**22**)

document 36

The death of Magellan

Magellan had led two boatloads of Spaniards in a foolhardy attack on the chief of the island of Mactan in the Philippines.

He then, in order to disperse this multitude and to terrify them, sent some of our men to set fire to their houses, but this rendered them more ferocious. Some of them ran to the fire, which consumed twenty or thirty houses, and there killed two of our men. The rest came down upon us with greater fury; they perceived that our bodies were defended, but that the legs were exposed, and they aimed at them principally. The captain had his right leg pierced by a poisoned arrow, on which account he gave orders to retreat by degrees; but almost all our men took to precipitate flight, so that there remained hardly six or eight of us with him. We were oppressed by the lances and stones which the enemy hurled at us, and we could make no more resistance. The bombards which we had in the boats were of no assistance to us, for the shoal water kept them too far from the beach. We went thither, retreating little by little, and still fighting, and we had already got to the distance of a crossbow shot from the shore, having the water up to our knees, the islanders following and picking up again the spears which they had already cast, and they threw the same spear five or six times; as they knew the captain they aimed specially at him, and twice they knocked the helmet off his head. He, with a few of us, like a good knight, remained at his post without choosing to retreat further. Thus we fought for more than an hour, until an Indian succeeded in thrusting a cane lance into the captain's face. He then, being irritated, pierced the Indian's breast with his lance, and left it in his body, and trying to draw his sword he was unable to draw it more than half way, on account of a javelin wound which he had received in the right arm. The enemies seeing this all rushed against him, and one of them with a great sword, like a great scimetar gave him a great blow on the left leg, which brought the captain down on his face, then the Indians threw themselves upon him, and ran him through with lances and scimetars, and all the other arms which they had, so that they deprived of life our mirror, light, comfort, and true guide. Whilst the Indians were thus overpowering him, several times he turned round towards us to see if we were all in safety, as though his obstinate fight had no other object than to give an opportunity for the retreat of his men. We who fought to extremity, and who were covered with wounds, seeing that he was dead, proceeded to the boats which were on the point of going away. This fatal battle was fought on the 27th of April of 1521, on a Saturday; a day which the captain had chosen himself, because he had a special devotion to it. There perished with him eight of our men, and four of the Indians, who had become Christians; we had also many wounded, amongst whom I must reckon myself. The enemy lost only fifteen men.

He died; but I hope that your illustrious highness[1] will not allow his memory to be lost, so much the more since I see revived in you the virtue of so great a captain, since one of his principal virtues was constance in the most adverse fortune. In the midst of the sea he was able to endure hunger better than we. Most versed in nautical charts, he knew better than any other the true art of navigation, of which it is a certain proof that he knew by his genius, and his intrepidity, without any one having given him the example, how to attempt the circuit of the globe, which he had almost completed.

[1] Charles V

From Antonio Pigafetta, *Magellan's First Voyage round the World*, trans. Lord Stanley of Alderney, Hakluyt Society, 1st series, LII, 1874, p. 100 (**22**)

document 37

A report on John Cabot

One of the few contemporary accounts of Cabot's motives, and of his voyage of 1497.

RAIMONDO DE SONCINO TO THE DUKE OF MILAN
[London, 18 December, 1497] Perhaps amid the numerous occupations of your Excellency, it may not weary you to hear how his Majesty here has gained a part of Asia, without a stroke of the sword. There is in this Kingdom a man of the people, Messer Zoane Caboto by name, of kindly wit and a most expert mariner. Having observed that the sovereigns first of Portugal and then of Spain had occupied unknown islands, he decided to make a similar acquisition for his Majesty. After obtaining patents that the effective ownership of what he might find should be his, though reserving the rights of the Crown, he committed himself to fortune in a little ship, with eighteen persons. He started from Bristol, a port on the west of this kingdom, passed Ireland, which is still further west, and then bore towards the north, in order to sail to the east, leaving the north on his right hand after some days. After having wandered for some time he at length arrived at the mainland, where he hoisted the royal standard, and took possession for the king here; and after taking certain tokens he returned.

This Messer Zoane, as a foreigner and a poor man, would not have obtained credence, had it not been that his companions, who are practically all English and from Bristol, testified that he spoke the truth. This Messer Zoane has the description of the world in a map, and also in a solid sphere, which he has made, and shows where he has been. In going towards the east he passed far beyond the country of the Tanais. They say that the land is excellent and temperate, and they believe that Brazil wood and silk are native there. They assert that the sea there is swarming with fish, which can be taken not only with the net, but in baskets let down with a stone, so that it sinks in the water. I have heard this Messer Zoane state so much.

These same English, his companions, say that they could bring so many fish that this kingdom would have no further need of Iceland, from which place there comes a very great quantity of the fish called stockfish. But Messer Zoane has his mind set upon even greater things, because he proposes to keep along the coast from the place at which he touched, more and more towards the east, until he reaches an island which he calls Cipango, situated in the equinoctial region, where he believes that all the spices of the world have their origin, as well as the jewels. He says that on previous occasions he has been to Mecca, whither spices are borne by caravans from distant countries. When he asked those who brought them what was the place of origin of these spices, they answered that they did not know, but that other caravans came with this merchandise to their homes from distant countries, and these again said that the goods had been brought to them from other remote regions. He therefore reasons that these things come from places far away from them, and so on from one to the other, always assuming that the earth is round, it follows as a matter of course that the last of all must take them in the north towards the west.

He tells all this in such a way, and makes everything so plain, that I also feel compelled to believe him. What is much more, his Majesty, who is wise and not prodigal, also gives him some credence, because he is giving him a fairly good provision, since his return, so Messer Zoane himself tells me. Before very long they say that his Majesty will equip some ships, and in addition he will give them all the malefactors, and they will go to that country and form a colony. By means of this they hope to make London a more important mart for spices than Alexandria. The leading men in this enterprise are from Bristol, and great seamen, and now they know where to go, say that the voyage will not take more than a fortnight, if they have good fortune after leaving Ireland.

I have also spoken with a Burgundian, one of Messer Zoane's companions, who corroborates everything. He wants to go back, because the Admiral, which is the name they give to Messer Zoane, has given him an island. He has given another to his barber, a Genoese by birth, and both consider themselves counts, while my lord the Admiral esteems himself at least a prince.

I also believe that some poor Italian friars will go on this voyage, who have the promise of bishoprics. As I have made friends with the Admiral, I might have an archbishopric if I chose to go there, but I have reflected that the benefices which your Excellency reserves for me are safer, and I therefore beg that possession may be given me of those which fall vacant in my absence, and the necessary steps taken so that they may not be taken away from me by others who have the advantage of being on the spot. Meanwhile I stay on in this country, eating ten or twelve courses at each meal, and spending three hours at table twice every day, for the love of your Excellency, to whom I humbly commend myself.

A letter from Raimondo de Soncino to the Duke of Milan, 18 Dec. 1497, in *Calendar of State Papers, Milan*, vol. I, no. 552, quoted in J. H. Parry (ed.), *The European Renaissance*, 1968, p. 280 (**20**)

document 38
A recently discovered letter about John Cabot

This undated letter, from an English merchant resident in Spain, possibly to Columbus, yields fresh information on Cabot. It was first published in 1957, having been found in the Spanish archives.

JOHN DAY TO THE LORD GRAND ADMIRAL
Your Lordship's servant brought me your letter. I have seen its contents and I would be most desirous and most happy to serve you. I do not find the book *Inventio Fortunata*, and I thought that I (or he) was bringing it with my things, and I am very sorry not to find it because I wanted very much to serve you. I am sending the other book of Marco Polo and a copy of the land which has been found. I do not send the map because I am not satisfied with it, for my many occupations forced me to make it in a hurry at the time of my departure; but from the said copy your Lordship will learn what you wish to know, for in it are named the capes of the mainland and the islands, and thus you will see where land was first sighted, since most of the land was discovered after turning back. Thus your Lordship will know that the cape nearest to Ireland is 1800 miles west of

Dursey Head which is in Ireland, and the southernmost part of the Island of the Seven Cities is west of Bordeaux River, and your Lordship will know that he landed at only one spot of the mainland, near the place where land was first sighted, and they disembarked there with a crucifix and raised banners with the arms of the Holy Father and those of the King of England, my master; and they found tall trees of the kind masts are made, and other fir trees, and the country is very rich in grass. In that particular spot, as I told your Lordship, they found a trail that went inland, they saw a site where a fire had been made, they saw manure of animals which they thought to be farm animals, and they saw a stick half a yard long pierced at both ends, carved and painted with brazil, and by such signs they believe the land to be inhabited. Since he was with just a few people, he did not dare advance inland beyond the shooting distance of a crossbow, and after taking in fresh water he returned to his ship. All along the coast they found many fish like those which in Iceland are dried in the open and sold in England and other countries, and these fish are called in England 'stockfish'; and thus following the shore they saw two forms running on land one after the other, but they could not tell if they were human beings or animals; and it seemed to them that there were fields where they thought might also be villages, and they saw a forest whose foliage looked red. They left England toward the end of May, and must have been on the way 35 days before sighting land; the wind was east-north-east and the sea calm going and coming back, except for one day when he ran into a storm two or three days before finding land; and going so far out, his compass needle failed to point north and marked two rhumbs below. They spent about one month discovering the coast and from the above mentioned cape of the mainland which is nearest to Ireland, they returned to the coast of Europe in fifteen days. They had the wind behind them, and he reached Brittany because the sailors confused him, saying that he was heading too far north. From there he came to Bristol, and he went to see the King to report to him all the above mentioned; and the King granted him an annual pension of twenty pounds sterling to sustain himself until the time comes when more will be known of this business, since with God's help it is hoped to push through plans for exploring the said land more thoroughly next year with ten or twelve vessels – because in his voyage he had only one ship of fifty 'toneles' and twenty men and food for seven or eight months – and they want to carry out this new project. It is considered certain that the cape of the said land was found and discovered in the past by the men from Bristol who found 'Brasil' as your Lordship well knows. It was called the Island of Brasil, and it is assumed and believed to be the mainland that the men from Bristol found.

Since your Lordship wants information relating to the first voyage, here is what happened: he went with one ship, he fell out with his crew, he was short of supplies and ran into bad weather, and he decided to turn back. . . .

Letter from John Day to the Lord Grand Admiral, ed. and trans. L. A. Vigneras, quoted in J. H. Parry (ed.) *The European Reconnaissance*, 1968, p. 280 **(20)**

document 39

Cartier's third voyage, 1540

Convinced by the Indians whom Cartier brought back from his second voyage that there was a rich empire in the interior of Canada, Francis I sends Cartier back once more to find it.

King Francis the first having heard the report of Captaine Cartier his Pilot generall in his two former Voyages of discovery, as well by writing as by word of mouth, touching that which hee had found and seene in the Westerne partes discovered by him in the parts of Canada and Hochelaga, and having also seene and talked with the people, which the sayd Cartier had brought out of those Countreys, whereof one was king of Canada, whose name was Donnacona, and others: which after that they had bene a long time in France and Britaine, were baptized at their owne desire and request, and died in the sayd countrey of Britaine. And albeit his Majestie was advertized by the sayd Cartier of the death and decease of all the people which were brought over by him (which were tenne in number) saving one little girle about tenne yeeres old, yet he resolved to send the sayd Cartier his Pilot thither againe, with John Francis de la Roche, Knight, Lord of Roberval, whome hee appointed his Lieutenant and Governour in the Countreys of Canada and Hochelaga, and the sayd Cartier Captaine generall and leader of the shippes, that they might discover more then was done before in the former voyages, and attaine (if it were possible) unto the knowledge of the Countrey of Saguenay, whereof the people brought by Cartier, as is declared, made mention unto the King, that there were great riches, and very good countreys. And the King caused a certaine summe of money to be delivered to furnish out the sayd voyage with five shippes: which thing was perfourmed by the sayd Monsieur Roberval and Cartier.

From Richard Hakluyt, *Principal Navigations*, 9 vols., 1928, vol. 8, p. 440 (**14**)

document 40

An encounter with civilization

Montaigne uses his meeting with Canadian Indians brought back to France by an explorer, in order to point up certain deficiencies in his own society.

Not knowing how costly a knowledge of this country's corruptions will one day be to their happiness and repose, and that from intercourse with us will come their ruin – which, I suppose, is far advanced already – three men of their nation – poor fellows to allow themselves to be deluded by the desire for things unknown, and to leave the softness of their own skies to come and gaze at ours – were at Rouen at the time when the late King Charles the Ninth visited the place. The King talked with them for some time: they were shown our way of living, our magnificence, and the sights of a fine city. Then someone asked them what they thought about all this, and what they had found most remarkable. They mentioned three things, of which I am sorry to say I have forgotten the third. But I still remember the other two. They said that in the first place they found it very strange that so many tall, bearded men, all strong and well armed, who were around the King – they probably meant the Swiss of his guard – should be willing to obey a child, rather than choose one of their own number to command them. Secondly – they have a way in their language of speaking of men as halves of one another – that they had noticed among us some men gorged to the full with things of every sort while their other halves were beggars at their doors, emaciated with hunger and poverty. They found it strange that these poverty stricken halves should suffer such injustice, and that they did not take the others by the throat or set fire to their houses.

From Michel de Montaigne, *Essays*, trans. J. M. Cohen, Penguin Books, 1958, p. 118

Chronology

127

1500	Juan de la Cosa's world map
1501	Vespucci's (?) second voyage
1502	Vasco da Gama's second voyage
1502	Columbus's last voyage
1504	Columbus's final return to Spain
1505	Almeida, first viceroy for India
1506	Death of Columbus
1508	Sebastian Cabot's voyage to North-West
1509	Battle of Diu
1509	Albuquerque, viceroy for India
1510	Capture of Goa
1511	Capture of Malacca
1513	Balboa sights Pacific
1519	Magellan's departure
1519	Cortés to Mexico
1521	Death of Magellan
1521	Siege and capture of Tenochtitlan
1522	El Cano's return to Spain
1524	Verrazzano's voyage to North America
1526	Sebastian Cabot's voyage to South America
1529	Treaty of Saragossa
1531	Pizarro to Peru
1531	Atahualpa captured at Cajamarca
1534	Cartier's first voyage
1535	Cartier's second voyage up St Lawrence River
1541	Cartier's third voyage
1542	Xavier to Goa
1543	First Portuguese visit to Japan
1545	Opening of silver mines at Potosi
1548	Sebastian Cabot to England
1550	Debate between Las Casas and Sepúlveda

Bibliography

This list is confined to works in English. A serious student of the Discoveries would need some facility in Spanish and Portuguese.

ORIGINAL SOURCES
(HS – Hakluyt Society)

1   Acosta, Fr. Joseph de, *The Natural and Moral History of the Indies*, HS, 1880
2   Azuara, G. E., *The Chronicle of the Discovery and Conquest of Guinea*, trans. C. R. Beazley and E. Prestage, HS, 2 vols., 1896–99
3   Badger, G. P., *The Travels of Ludovico de Varthema*, HS, 1863
4   Biggar, H. P., *The Voyages of Jacques Cartier*, Ottawa, 1924
5   Blake, J. B., *Europeans in West Africa 1450–1560*, HS, 2 vols., 1942–44
6   Camoens, L. V. de, *The Lusiads*, trans. W. C. Atkinson, Penguin, 1952
7   Correa, Gaspar, *Lendas da India*, HS, 1869
8   Crone, G. R. (ed.), *The Voyages of Cadamosto*, HS, 1937
9   Daines, M. L. (ed.), *The Book of Duarte Barbosa*, HS, 2 vols., 1918–21
10 Davenport, F. G., (ed.) *European Treaties Bearing upon the History of the United States*, 4 vols., Washington, 1917–37
11 Díaz, Bernal (del Castillo), *The True History of the Conquest of New Spain*, 5 vols., HS, 1908–16
12 Elton, G. R., *Renaissance and Reformation 1300–1648*, Collier Macmillan, 1963
13 Greenlee, W. B., *The Voyages of Pedro Alvares Cabral to Brazil and India*, HS, 1938
14 Hakluyt, Richard, *Principal Navigations*, 9 vols., 1928
15 Jayne, C., *Select Documents Illustrating the Four Voyages of Columbus*, 2 vols., HS, 1930–33
16 *Mandeville's Travels*, 2 vols., HS, 1950–53
17 Markham, C. R. (ed.), *The Journal of Christopher Columbus During his First Voyage 1492–93*, HS, 1893

Bibliography

18   Morison, S. E., *Journals and Other Documents on the Life and Voyages of Christopher Columbus*, New York, 1963

19   Olson, J. E., and Bourne, E. G., (eds.), *The Northmen, Columbus and Cabot 985–1503*, New York, 1959

20   Parry, J. H., *The European Reconnaissance, Selected Documents*, Macmillan, 1968

21   Pereira, Duarte Pacheo, *Esmeraldo de situ orbe*, HS, 1937

22   Pigafetta, Antonio, *Magellan's First Voyage round the World*, trans. Lord Stanley of Alderney, HS 1874

23   Ravenstein, E. G., (ed.), *First Voyage of Vasco da Gama*, HS, 1898

24   Vespucci, Amerigo, *Letters of Amerigo Vespucci*, ed. Markham, C. R., HS, 1894

25   Wroth, Lawrence C., *The Voyages of Giovanni da Verrazzano, 1524–1528*, Yale, 1970

26   Xeres, Francisco de, *Reports on the Discovery of Peru*, ed. Markham, C. R., HS, 1872

SECONDARY SOURCES

27   Axelson, Eric, *Congo to Cape*, Faber 1973

28   Boxer, C. R., *The Portuguese Seaborne Empire 1415–1825*, Hutchinson, 1977

29   Brebner, J. B., *The Explorers of North America 1492–1806*, Black, 1965

30   Chaunu, P., *European Expansion in the later Middle Ages*, North Holland Publishing Co., 1979

31   Cipolla, C. M., *European Culture and Overseas Expansion*, Penguin, 1970

32   Cortesao, A., *The Mystery of Vasco da Gama*, Coimbra, 1973

33   Crone, G. R., *Maps and Their Makers*, Dawson, 1953

34   Crone, G. R., *The Discovery of America*, Hamish Hamilton 1969

35   Diffie, B. W. and Winius, G. D., *Foundations of the Portuguese Empire 1415–1580*, Oxford University Press 1977

36   Elliott, J. H., *The Old World and the New 1492–1650*, Cambridge University Press 1972

37   Elton, G. R. (ed.), *The New Cambridge Modern History, vol. II: The Reformation 1520–1553*, Cambridge University Press, 1958

38   Hale, J. R., *Renaissance Exploration*, BBC, 1968

39   Hanke, Lewis, *The Spanish Struggle for Justice in the Conquest of America*, University of Pennsylvania Press, 1950

40   Hanke, Lewis, *Aristotle and the American Indians*, Indiana University Press, 1959

41 Hemming, J., *The Conquest of the Incas*, Macmillan, 1970

42 Hoffman, B. G., *Cabot to Cartier*, Toronto, 1961

43 Jayne, K. G., *Vasco da Gama and his Successors, 1460–1580*, 1910

44 Jensen, De Lamar, (ed.), *The Expansion of Europe, Motives, Methods and Meanings*, D. C. Heath and Co., 1967

45 Kirkpatrick, A., *The Spanish Conquistadores*, 1934

46 Lack, D. F., *Asia in the Making of Europe, vol. I: The Century of Discovery*, Chicago, 1965 (2 books)

47 Merriman, R. B., *The Rise of the Spanish Empire in the Old World and in the New*, 3 vols., New York, 1962

48 Morison, S. E., *Christopher Columbus, Admiral of the Ocean Sea*, Oxford University Press, 1942

49 Morison, S. E., *Portuguese Voyages to America in the Fifteenth Century*, Octagon, 1965

50 Morison, S. E., *The European Discovery of America : vol. I, The Northern Voyages A. D. 500–1600*, Oxford University Press, 1971

51 Morison, S. E., *The European Discovery of America : vol. II, The Southern Voyages 1492–1616*, Oxford University Press, 1974

52 O'Gorman, E., *The Invention of America*, Greenwood, 1961

53 Panikkar, K. M., *Asia and Western Dominance*, Allen and Unwin, 1959

54 Parry, J. H., *The Age of Reconnaissance*, Weidenfeld and Nicolson, 1963

55 Parry, J. H., *The Spanish Seaborne Empire*, Hutchinson, 1977

56 Parry, J. H., *The Discovery of the Sea*, Weidenfeld and Nicolson, 1975

57 Pohl, F. J., *Amerigo Vespucci; Pilot Major*, Octagon, 1944

58 Potter, G. R., (ed.), *The New Cambridge Modern History, vol. I: The Renaissance 1493–1520*, Cambridge University Press, 1971

59 Penrose, Boes, *Travel and Discovery in the Renaissance 1420–1620*, Harvard, 1960

60 Prestage, Edgar, *The Portuguese Pioneers*, 1933

61 Quinn, D. B., *England and the Discovery of America 1481–1620*, Knopf, 1974

62 Ravenstein, E. G., *Martin Behaim, His Life and His Globe*, 1908

63 Skelton, R. A., *Explorers' Maps*, Routledge and Kegan Paul, 1958

64 Taylor, E. G. R., *The Haven-Finding Art*, Hollis, 1971

65 Webb, Walter Prescott, *The Great Frontier*, University of Texas, 1964

66 Williamson, J. A., *The Cabot Voyages and Bristol Discovery under Henry VII*, HS, 1961

67 Yates, Frances A., *Astraea: The Imperial Theme in the Sixteenth Century*, Routledge and Kegan Paul, 1975

ARTICLES

68 Axelson, Eric, 'Prince Henry the Navigator and the Discovery of the Sea Route to India', *Geographical Journal*, CXXVII, pt. 2, June 1961, pp. 145–58

69 Campbell, Eila, 'Verdict on the Vinland Map', *Geographical Magazine*, April 1974, p. 307

70 Cook, Harold J., 'Ancient Wisdom, the Golden Age and Atlantis: the New World in Sixteenth Century Cosmology', *Terrae Incognitae*, X, 1978, pp. 25–43

71 Cortada, James W., 'Myths, Facts and Debates: Christopher Columbus and the New World before 1492', *Renaissance and Reformation*, XII, 1976, pp. 89–96

72 Davies, Arthur, 'The Date of Juan de la Cosa's World Map', *Geographical Journal*, 142, 1976, pp. 112–16

73 Davies, Arthur, 'Columbus the Admiral', *Geographical Magazine*, Dec. 1976

74 Davies, Arthur, 'Behaim, Martellus and Columbus', *Geographical Journal*, 143, 1977, pp. 451–7

75 Davies, Arthur, 'Magellan and his Grand Design', *Geographical Magazine*, Oct. 1979

76 Diffie, Bailey W., 'Foreigners in Portugal and the "Policy of Silence"', *Terrae Incognitae*, I, 1969, pp. 23–34

77 Elliott, J. H., 'The Mental World of Hernán Cortés', *Transactions of the Royal Historical Society*, 5th series, XVII, 1967, pp. 41–58

78 Elliott, J. H., 'Renaissance Europe and America: a blunted impact?', in *First Images of America*, vol. I, ed. Chiapelli, F., Univ. of California, 1976, pp. 11–22

79 Goldstein, Thomas, 'Geography in Fifteenth-Century Florence', in Parker, J. (ed.), *Merchants and Scholars : Essays in the History of Exploration and Trade*, Minneapolis, 1965

80 Hale, J. R., 'A World Elsewhere', in Hay, D. (ed.), *The Age of the Renaissance*, Thames and Hudson, 1967

81 Letts, M., 'Prester John', *Transactions of the Royal Historical Society*, 4th series, XXIX, 1947, pp. 19–26

82 Mattingly, G., 'No Peace beyond what Line?' *Transactions of the Royal Historical Society*, 5th series, XIII, 1963, pp. 145–62

83 McGrath, Patrick, 'Bristol and America 1480–1631', in Andrews, K. R. (ed.), *The Westward Enterprise*, 1978

84 Morison, S. E., 'The Sailing Instructions of Vasco da Gama to Cabral', *The Mariner's Mirror*, XXIV, 1938, pp. 402–7

85 Morton, R. Nance, 'The Ship of the Renaissance', *The Mariner's Mirror*, XLI, 1955, pp. 180–92

86 Parry, J. H., 'The Navigators of the Conquista', *Terrae Incognitae*, X, 1978, pp. 61–70

87 Parry, J. H., 'Asia-in-the-West', *Terrae Incognitae*, VIII, 1976, pp. 59–70

88 Prause, Gerhard, 'Columbus on a Secret Mission?', *Encounter*, April 1973, pp. 59–63

89 Quinn, D. B., 'Renaissance Influences in English Colonization', *Transactions of the Royal Historical Society*, 5th series, XXVI, 1976, pp. 73–93

90 Ruddock, Alwyn A., 'Columbus and Iceland', *Geographical Journal*, CXXXVI, 1970, pp. 176–89

91 Ruddock, Alwyn A., 'The Reputation of Sebastian Cabot', *Bulletin of the Institute of Historical Research*, 47, 1974, pp. 95–8

92 Scammell, G. V., 'The New Worlds and Europe in the Sixteenth Century', *The Historical Journal*, XII, 3, 1963, pp. 389–412

93 Solver, C. V. and Marcus, G. J., 'Dead Reckoning and the Ocean Voyages of the Past', *The Mariner's Mirror*, XLIV, 1958, pp. 18–34

94 Williamson, J. A., 'The Voyages of Sebastian Cabot', *Historical Association Pamphlet*, 106, 1937

Index